CHILDREN'S
ATLAS

David and Jill Wright

BCA

LONDON NEW YORK SYDNEY TORONTO

CONTENTS

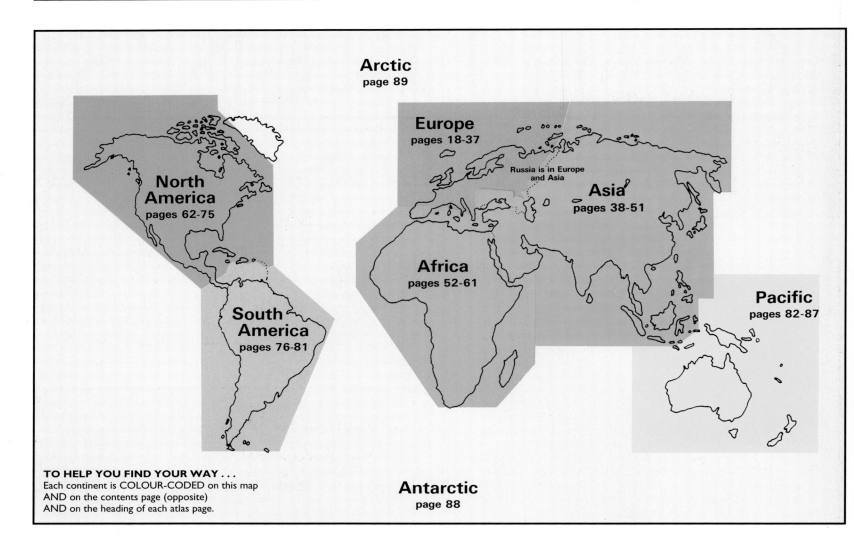

Arctic
page 89

Europe
pages 18-37

Russia is in Europe
and Asia

Asia
pages 38-51

North America
pages 62-75

Africa
pages 52-61

Pacific
pages 82-87

South America
pages 76-81

TO HELP YOU FIND YOUR WAY . . .
Each continent is COLOUR-CODED on this map
AND on the contents page (opposite)
AND on the heading of each atlas page.

Antarctic
page 88

To Rachel and Steven

This edition published 1994
by BCA by arrangement with
George Philip Limited,
an imprint of Reed Consumer Books Limited

Text ©1994 David and Jill Wright
Maps ©1994 Reed International Books
Limited

Cartography by Philip's

CN 1605

Printed in Italy

Front Cover – Children of the World
These children live in Australia (top left:
Tony Stone Images/Paul Chesley); Japan (top
right: Tony Stone Images); Thailand (bottom
left: Tony Stone Images/Ian Murphy); and
Mozambique (bottom right: Still Pictures/
Jorgen Schytte). The flags of Swaziland (left)
and Brunei (right) are illustrated at the top.

Back Cover
Market Day in Bida (see page 56)
Wind-pumps in the Netherlands (see page 25)

OUR PLANET EARTH

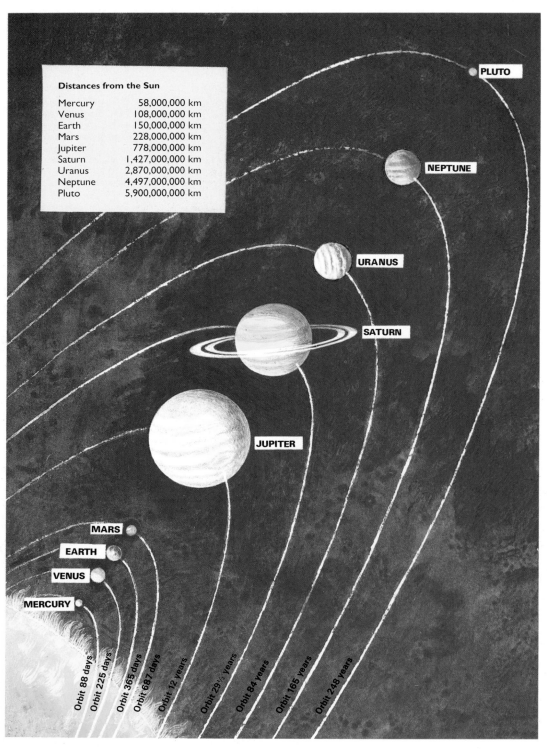

Distances from the Sun

Mercury	58,000,000 km
Venus	108,000,000 km
Earth	150,000,000 km
Mars	228,000,000 km
Jupiter	778,000,000 km
Saturn	1,427,000,000 km
Uranus	2,870,000,000 km
Neptune	4,497,000,000 km
Pluto	5,900,000,000 km

PLUTO

NEPTUNE

URANUS

SATURN

JUPITER

MARS

EARTH

VENUS

MERCURY

Orbit 88 days

Orbit 225 days

Orbit 365 days

Orbit 687 days

Orbit 12 years

Orbit 29½ years

Orbit 84 years

Orbit 165 years

Orbit 248 years

◀ *Our planet Earth is one of nine planets that travel round the Sun. This diagram shows that we are 150 million kilometres away from the Sun.*

It takes 365¼ days for the Earth to travel all the way round the Sun, which we call a year. Every four years we add an extra day to February to use up the ¼ days. This is called a Leap Year. The Earth travels at a speed of over 107,000 kilometres an hour. (You have travelled 600 kilometres through space while reading this!)

As the Earth travels through space, it is also spinning round and round. It spins round once in 24 hours, which we call a day. Places on the Equator are spinning at 1660 kilometres an hour. Because of the way the Earth spins, we experience day and night, and different seasons during a year (see page 13). No part of our planet is too hot or too cold for life to survive.

Our nearest neighbour in space is the Moon, 384,400 kilometres away. The first men to reach the Moon took four days to travel there in 1969. On the way, they took photographs of the Earth, such as the one on the right. The Earth looks very blue from space because of all the sea. It is the only planet in the Solar System with sea. Look at the swirls of cloud, especially over southern Africa and over northern Europe. These show that the Earth has an atmosphere. Our atmosphere contains oxygen and water vapour and it keeps us and all other living things alive.

Fact box: Earth

Distance around the Equator 40,075 kilometres

Distance around the poles 40,007 kilometres

Distance to the centre of the Earth 6370 kilometres

Surface area of the Earth 510,065,600 square kilometres (71% sea; 29% land)

Distance from the Earth to the Sun 150,000,000 kilometres (It takes 8½ minutes for the Sun's light to reach the Earth.)

Distance from the Earth to the Moon 384,400 kilometres

The Earth travels around the Sun at 107,000 kilometres per hour, or 29.8 kilometres per second

The Earth's atmosphere is about 175 kilometres thick

The chief gases in the atmosphere are nitrogen (78%) and oxygen (21%)

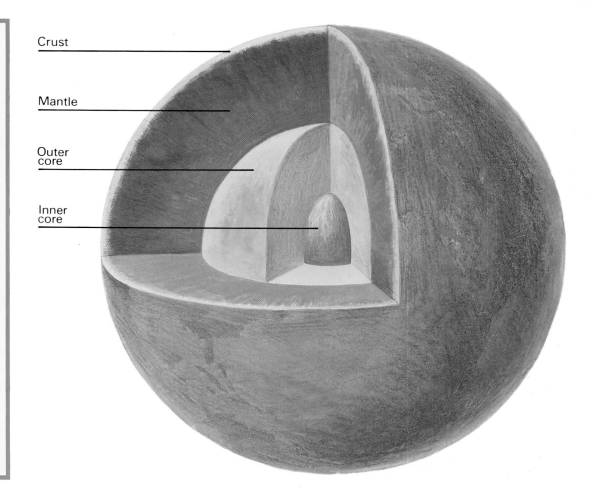

Crust

Mantle

Outer core

Inner core

Scientists tell us our Earth is made of layers of rock. The diagram above shows the Earth with a slice cut out. The hottest part is the core, at the centre. Around the core is the mantle. The outer layer, the crust, is quite thin under the oceans, but it is thicker under the continents. Scientists now know that the Earth's crust is cracked, like the shell of a hard-boiled egg that has been dropped. The cracks are called faults. The huge sections of crust divided by the faults are called plates and they are moving very, very slowly. The continents have gradually moved across the Earth's surface as the crustal plates have moved. Sudden movements near the faults cause earthquakes or volcanic eruptions.

◀ *This satellite photo* shows Africa and part of South America. These two continents were joined together, but about 100 million years ago they began to split apart.

MOUNTAINS, PLAINS AND SEAS

The map shows that there is much more sea than land in the world. The Pacific is by far the biggest ocean; the map splits it in two.

Mountains are shown in relief on this map. Look for the world's highest mountain range – the Himalayas, in Asia. There are high mountains on the western side of both American continents. Most of the world's great mountain ranges have been made by folding in the Earth's crust.

Desert areas are shown in orange. The green expanse across northern Europe and northern Asia is the world's biggest plain.

▼ *Part of the Great Plains of North America.* *The land is flat as far as the eye can see, but it is also 1000 metres above sea level – plains are not always lowland.*

Greenland

Rocky Mountains

Great Plains

North America

Grand Canyon

Mississippi

Appalachian Mountains

ATLANTIC OCEAN

P A C I F I C O C E A N

Tropic of Cancer

Equator

Tropic of Capricorn

180°

180°

Angel Falls

Amazon

Andes

South America

Scale along the equator 1:116 000 000

0   1000km 2000km 3000km 4000km 5000km

1cm on the map = 1160 kilometres on the ground

0   1000 miles   2000 miles   3000 miles

1 inch on the map = 1860 miles on the ground

Fact box

Highest mountain Mount Everest, 8848 metres (Asia)
Longest mountain range Andes, 7200 kilometres (South America)
Longest rivers Nile, 6670 kilometres (Africa); Amazon, 6448 kilometres (South America)

Longest gorge Grand Canyon, 349 kilometres (North America)
Highest waterfall Angel Falls, 979 metres (Venezuela, South America)
Largest lake Caspian Sea, 360,700 square kilometres (Europe and Asia)
Deepest lake Lake Baykal, 1940 metres (Russia)

Largest ocean Pacific, 181,000,000 square kilometres
Deepest part of oceans Mariana Trench, 11,022 metres (Pacific)
Largest islands Australia, 7,686,848 square kilometres; Greenland, 2,175,600 square kilometres
Largest desert Sahara, 8,400,000 square kilometres (Africa)

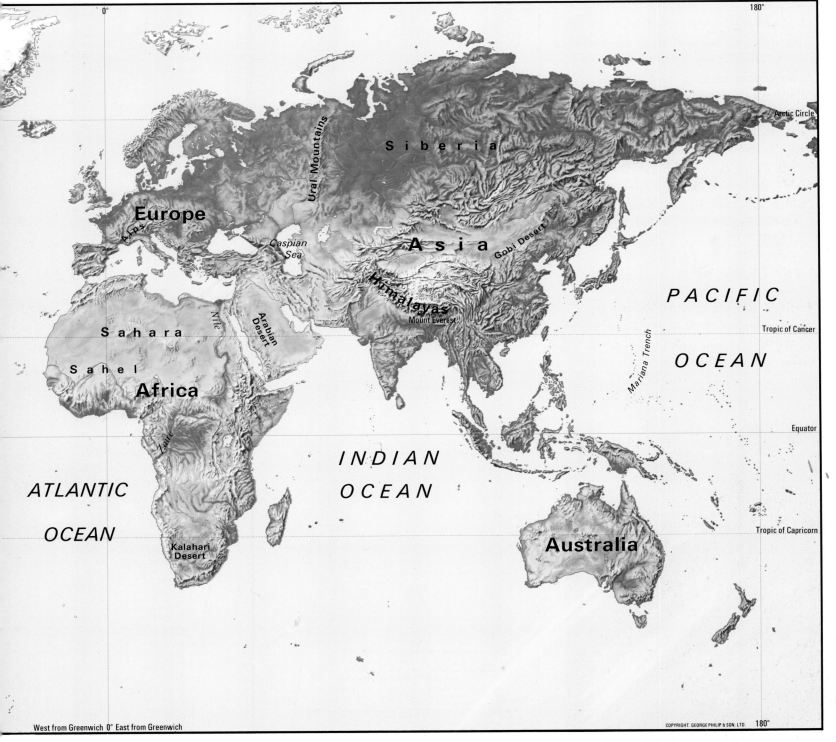

West from Greenwich 0° East from Greenwich

180°

COUNTRIES OF THE WORLD

Five of the continents of the world are divided into countries. Most countries are now independent and manage their own affairs. A few of the smaller countries and islands are still ruled by another country.

Look at the boundaries between countries. Some follow natural features, such as rivers or mountain ranges. Straight boundaries were drawn for convenience. Often they separate people of the same language or tribe, and this can create problems.

▼ **The United Nations building,** in New York City, USA. The world's problems are discussed here – and sometimes solved. Almost every country has a representative at the United Nations.

Greenland

RUSSIA

Alaska (U.S.A.)

CANADA

UNITED STATES OF AMERICA (U.S.A.)

Bermuda

Tropic of Cancer

BAHAMAS

Hawaiian Islands

MEXICO

CUBA

JAMAICA

DOMINICAN REPUBLIC

BELIZE

HAITI

PUERTO RICO

HONDURAS

GUATEMALA

EL SALVADOR

NICARAGUA

TRINIDAD & TOBAGO

COSTA RICA

VENEZUELA

GUYANA

PANAMA

SURINAM

COLOMBIA

French Guiana

Equator

ECUADOR

BRAZIL

PERU

BOLIVIA

FRENCH POLYNESIA

Tropic of Capricorn

PARAGUAY

CHILE

URUGUAY

ARGENTINA

KEY

ARM. = ARMENIA	LUX. = LUXEMBOURG
AZER. = AZERBAIJAN	MAC. = MACEDONIA
B. = BHUTAN	MOL. = MOLDAVIA
B.-H. = BOSNIA HERZEGOVINA	N. = NETHERLANDS
BUR. = BURUNDI	R. = RWANDA
BEL. = BELGIUM	SL. = SLOVENIA
CRO. = CROATIA	S. = SWITZERLAND
L. = LEBANON	U.A.E. = UNITED ARAB EMIRATES
LITH. = LITHUANIA	YUGO. = YUGOSLAVIA

Falkland Islands

South Georgia

Scale along the equator 1:116 000 000

```
0    1000km  2000km  3000km  4000km  5000km
```
1cm on the map = 1160 kilometres on the ground
```
0         1000miles      2000miles     3000miles
```
1inch on the map = 1860miles on the ground

Fact box

Only five of the 'top ten' countries with large populations are also among the 'top ten' biggest countries.

Asia has 6½★ of the ten most populated countries – but only 2½★ of the 'top ten' biggest countries. (★Russia is in both Asia and Europe.)

Top ten countries by size (square kilometres)

1	Russia	17,075,000	6	Australia	7,686,848
2	Canada	9,976,140	7	India	3,287,590
3	China	9,597,000	8	Argentina	2,776,889
4	USA	9,363,123	9	Kazakhstan	2,717,300
5	Brazil	8,511,965	10	Sudan	2,505,813

Top ten countries by population (UN figures)

1	China	1,134 million	6	Russia	147 million
2	India	854 million	7	Japan	124 million
3	USA	252 million	8	Nigeria	119 million
4	Indonesia	190 million	9	Bangladesh	115 million
5	Brazil	151 million	10	Pakistan	115 million

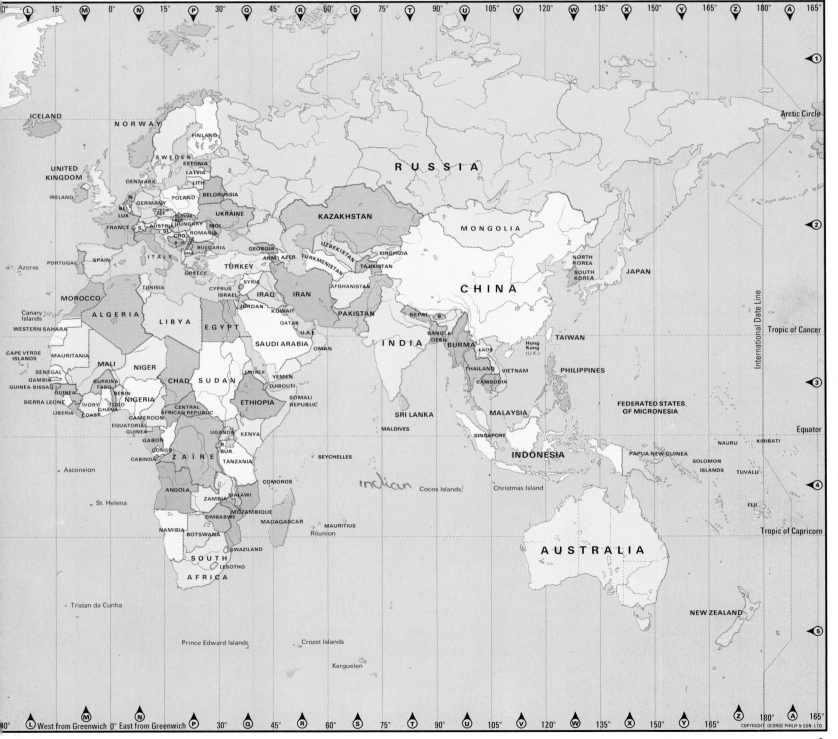

PEOPLE OF THE WORLD

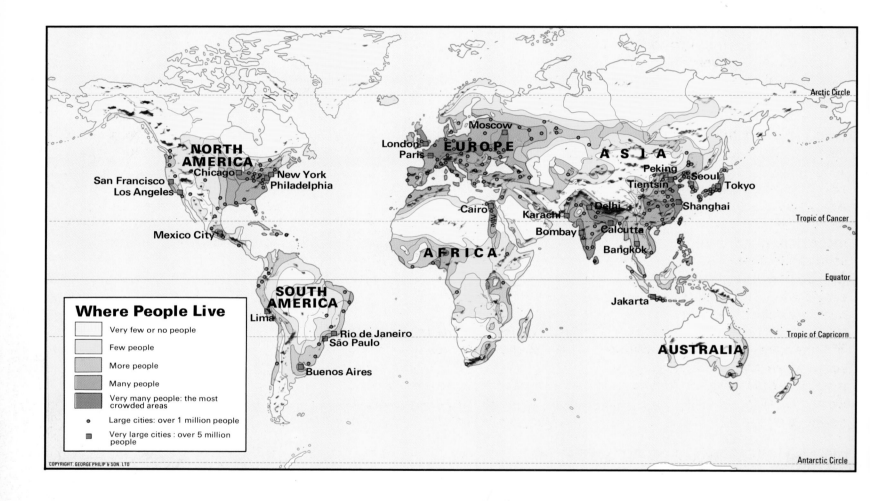

Where People Live

- Very few or no people
- Few people
- More people
- Many people
- Very many people: the most crowded areas
- ○ Large cities: over 1 million people
- ■ Very large cities : over 5 million people

COPYRIGHT. GEORGE PHILIP & SON. LTD

There is *one* race of people: the human race. In Latin, we are all known as *Homo sapiens* – 'wise person'. The differences between people, such as dark or light skin, hair and eyes, are small. This map shows where the world's people live. Most of the world has very few people: large areas are shown in yellow. Compare these areas with the maps on pages 6–7 and 15 and you will see that they are mostly desert, or high mountains, or densely forested, or very cold.

Over half the world's people live in the lowlands of south and east Asia. Other crowded areas are parts of north-west Europe, the Nile Valley and north-east USA. The most crowded places of all are the big cities.

▶ **Watering onions in the Gambia, West Africa.** *This boy's watering-can was given by a charity, to help the family grow more food. Many schemes like this are helped by money from people in the rich countries of the world.*

The smaller map (right) shows the rich and poor countries of the world. In any one country there are rich and poor people, but the difference between countries is even greater.

The map shows that the richest countries are in North America, north-west Europe, parts of the Middle East, Japan and Australia. Here, most people usually get enough to eat. They can buy a variety of different foods; they can go to a doctor or hospital when they need to, and the children can go to school.

The poorest countries (shown in dark green) are in the Tropics – especially in Africa and south Asia. Life in these countries is very different from life in the rich world. Many people struggle to grow enough food, and they are often hungry. People who do not have enough to eat find it difficult to work hard and they get ill more easily. They do not have enough money to pay for medicines or to send their children to school to learn to read and write. Some of the poorest people live in shanty towns in or near large cities (see below).

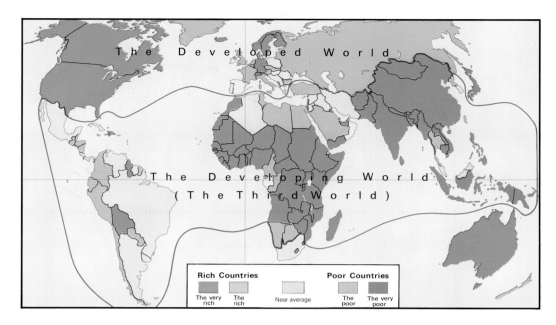

Rich Countries

The very rich The rich Near average

Poor Countries

The poor The very poor

▲ **Empty and poor: nomads in the Sahara.** *Bedouin nomads drink a cup of tea in the Sahara Desert. Most of the world's deserts are empty except where crops can be irrigated or minerals can be mined.*

▼ **Crowded and rich: New York City.** *The offices of Manhattan Island, in the centre of New York, are crowded with workers during the day, but are empty at night. Only the richest people can afford to live in apartments here.*

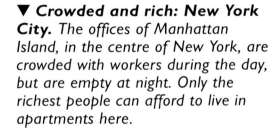

▼ **Crowded and poor: a shanty town in Brazil.** *These shanties on a steep hillside in Rio de Janeiro were built by people who have nowhere else to live.*

HOT AND COLD LANDS

Five important lines are drawn across these maps of the world: the Arctic and Antarctic Circles; the Tropics of Cancer and Capricorn; and the Equator. They divide the world roughly into the *polar*, *temperate* and *tropical* zones.

◀ *Arctic winter.* Winter begins early in Greenland. These fishing boats are frozen in the harbour at Angmagssalik. From late September the days get shorter, until there are 24 hours of dark and cold at Christmastime.

The *polar* lands remain cold all through the year, even though the summer days are long and some snow melts.

The *temperate* lands have four seasons: summer and winter, with spring and autumn in between. But these seasons come at different times of the year north and south of the Equator.

The *tropical* lands are always hot, except where mountains or plateaus reach high above sea-level. For some of the year the sun is directly overhead.

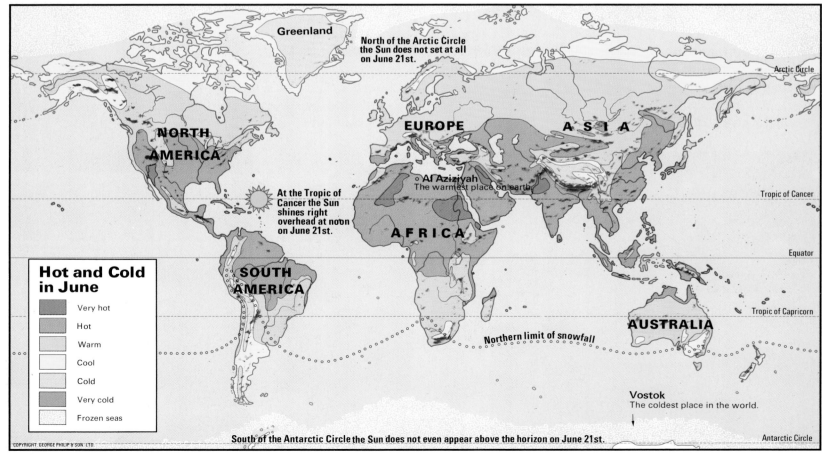

Greenland

North of the Arctic Circle the Sun does not set at all on June 21st.

Arctic Circle

NORTH AMERICA

EUROPE

ASIA

At the Tropic of Cancer the Sun shines right overhead at noon on June 21st.

Al Aziziyah
The warmest place on earth

Tropic of Cancer

AFRICA

Equator

SOUTH AMERICA

AUSTRALIA

Tropic of Capricorn

Northern limit of snowfall

Vostok
The coldest place in the world.

Hot and Cold in June

- Very hot
- Hot
- Warm
- Cool
- Cold
- Very cold
- Frozen seas

South of the Antarctic Circle the Sun does not even appear above the horizon on June 21st.

Antarctic Circle

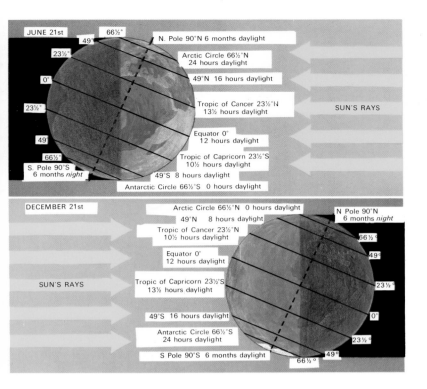

The diagrams above help to explain why the seasons vary north and south of the Equator. In June (top) the sun is overhead at the Tropic of Cancer. The North Pole is tilted towards the sun, and the Arctic enjoys 24 hours of daylight. It is summer in North America, Europe and Asia. Notice that Antarctica is in total darkness.

By December, the Earth has travelled half way round the sun. Spot the difference in December (below). Where is the sun overhead? Now Antarctica has 24 hours of daylight. It is summer in the southern continents, so children in Australia open Christmas presents in their summer holidays (see page 85).

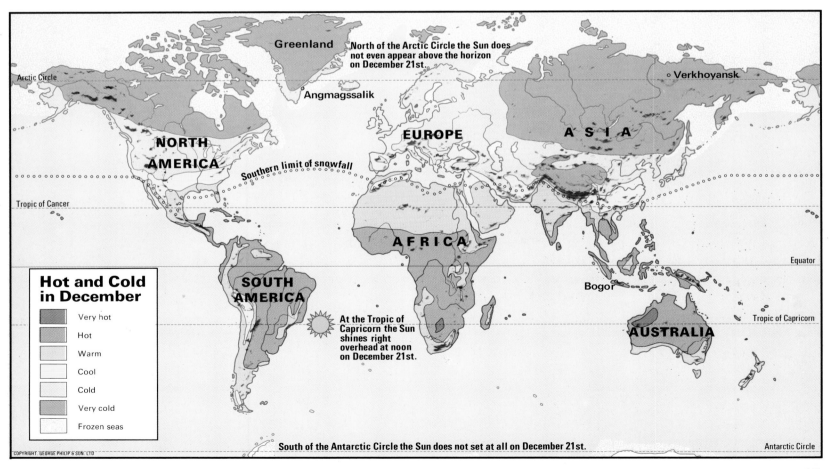

Hot and Cold in December

- Very hot
- Hot
- Warm
- Cool
- Cold
- Very cold
- Frozen seas

WET AND DRY LANDS

▲ **Burning the savanna,** in northern Ghana, West Africa. At the end of the long dry season, farmers burn the bush (long grass and small trees). The land will be ready for planting crops as soon as the wet season begins.

Water is needed by all living things. The map below shows that different parts of the world receive different amounts of water. Follow the Equator: most places near the Equator are very wet as well as being very hot. The map opposite shows that near the Equator there are large areas of thick forest. Here, it rains almost every day. Now follow the Tropic of Cancer and the Tropic of Capricorn on both maps. The Tropics cross areas of desert, where it is dry all year. Between the desert and the forest is an area of tall grass and bushes called the savanna. People here talk about the 'wet' and 'dry' seasons. For part of the year it is as rainy as at the Equator; for the rest of the year it is as dry as the desert.

North of the Sahara Desert is the Mediterranean Sea. Places around this sea have lovely hot, dry summers, but they do have rain in winter. There are areas near other deserts with a similar climate, such as California in North America and central Chile in South America.

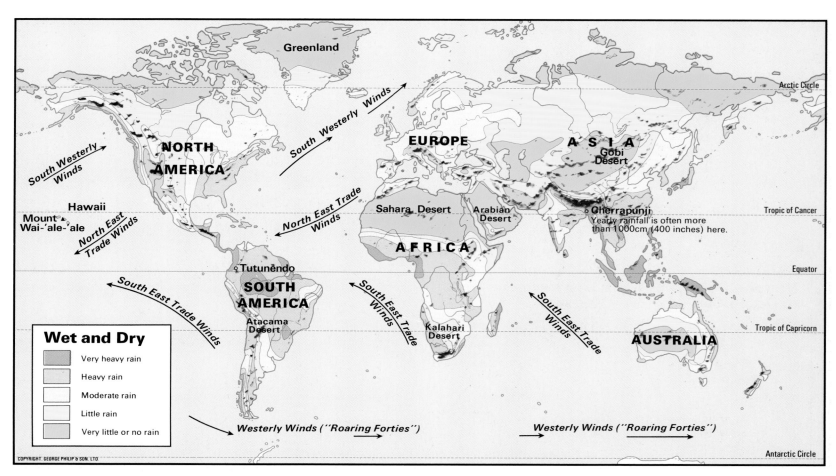

Wet and Dry

- Very heavy rain
- Heavy rain
- Moderate rain
- Little rain
- Very little or no rain

COPYRIGHT. GEORGE PHILIP & SON. LTD.

◀ *Forest and mountains* in Alberta, Canada. The coniferous trees can survive Canada's bitterly cold winters. In the high mountains, trees cannot grow: it is too cold and the soil is too thin. Similar forests stretch across northern Europe and Asia, in Scandinavia and Siberia. The wood may be used for paper for books.

▼ *Desert in Namibia,* southern Africa. The Namib Desert has given its name to the country of Namibia. It is a very dry area, west of the Kalahari Desert. Winds usually blow away from the land, so rain is very rare.

In the temperate lands, many places have some rain all through the year. Damp winds from the sea bring plenty of rain to the coastal areas, and trees grow well. London and New York have some rain every month. Far inland, near the centre of the continents, and where high mountains cut off the sea winds, it is much drier. Here, there are vast grasslands, like the prairies of North America.

The Arctic and Antarctic lands are nearly as dry as the hot deserts. But the moisture collects as snow. Where the snow melts in the short summer, flowers and small plants grow in the marshy soil — called the tundra.

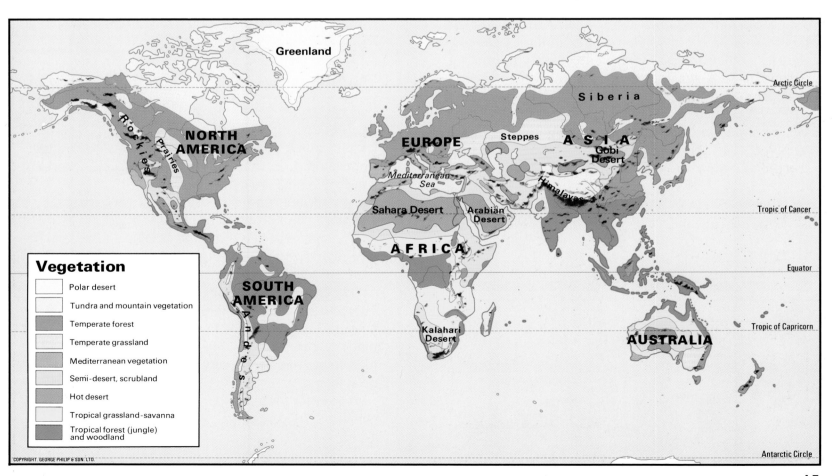

Vegetation

- Polar desert
- Tundra and mountain vegetation
- Temperate forest
- Temperate grassland
- Mediterranean vegetation
- Semi-desert, scrubland
- Hot desert
- Tropical grassland-savanna
- Tropical forest (jungle) and woodland

COPYRIGHT. GEORGE PHILIP & SON. LTD.

Greenland

Arctic Circle

Siberia

NORTH AMERICA

EUROPE

Steppes

ASIA

Gobi Desert

Rockies

Prairies

Mediterranean Sea

Himalayas

Sahara Desert

Arabian Desert

Tropic of Cancer

AFRICA

Equator

SOUTH AMERICA

Andes

Kalahari Desert

Tropic of Capricorn

AUSTRALIA

Antarctic Circle

ENJOYING MAPS

The world maps (pages 6 to 15). Because the world is round, the best model is a globe. It is impossible to draw a really accurate map of the round world on a flat piece of paper. The world maps on pages 6 to 10 and 12 to 15 have the right *shape* for the land, but the *size* of northern lands is too big. The map on page 11 has the wrong *shapes* but the *size* is right: it is an *'equal-area'* map. Try comparing Alaska or New Zealand on the two maps. Which world map do you prefer?

The area maps (pages 18 to 89). These maps show the continents and countries of the world. Each map has a key, with information that will help you 'read' the map. Use your imagination to 'see' what the land is like in each part of the world that you visit through these pages. The photos and text will make your picture clearer.

These two pages explain the key to all the maps. The country of Ghana is used as an example. Ghana is in

▼ *The border between Ghana and Burkina Faso.*
The red lines on the map show the boundaries between countries. When travelling from one country to another, you have to stop at the border. These children live in Ghana and their flag flies on their side of the border.

'BYE-BYE SAFE JOURNEY' is the message on the arch. In Ghana, most officials speak English, and people drive on the left. But in Burkina Faso officials speak French and people drive on the right.

square B2 of the map (right). Find ⊕ at the top of the map with one finger, and ②► at the side of the map with another finger. Move each finger in the direction of the arrows; Ghana is where they meet. The stamps and photograph on this page come from Ghana.

The capital city of each country is underlined on the maps. The rulers of the country live in the capital city, and it is the biggest city in most countries. But not all capital cities are big. On this map, you can see three sizes of city. The biggest ones are marked by a square; they have over one million people. Middle-sized cities have a big dot, and smaller cities have a small dot. Small towns and villages are not shown on maps of this scale, but some have been included in this atlas because they are mentioned in the text.

Countries that are coloured bright yellow on the map are shown in more detail on other pages. The small inset map shows where the main map fits into the continent of Africa. Maps of the whole of Africa are at the beginning of the Africa section (pages 52–3).

This is your chance to explore Africa – enjoy yourself!

Postage stamps

Postage stamps are on many pages of this atlas. You can learn so much from stamps! For example: the map shows you that Ghana is a country; the stamps tell you the official language of Ghana, and show you Ghana's flag.

The map tells you the name of Ghana's biggest lake (man-made). The 6Np stamp shows you the dam and tells you its name.

The map tells you that Ghana has a coastline; the 10Np stamp tells you the name of Ghana's main port, and shows you the big modern cranes there. The map shows this port is very near Accra.

Np stands for new pesewas (100 pesewas = 1 cedi).

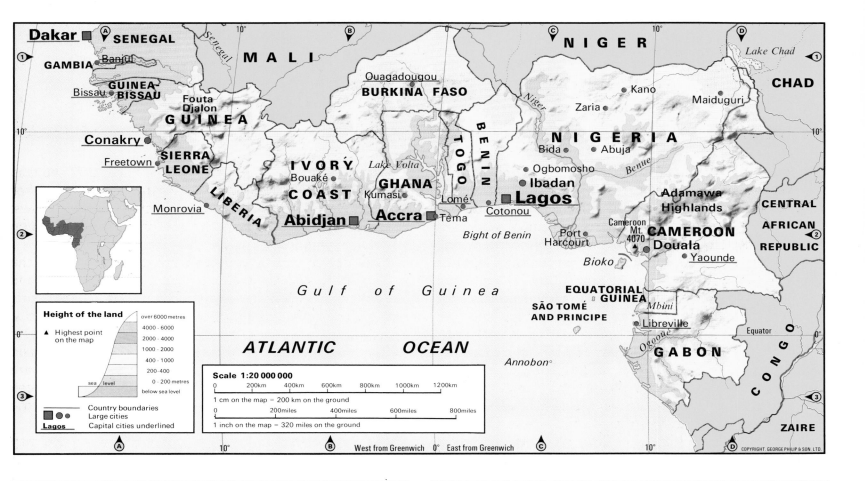

Scale

Scale 1:20 000 000

| 0 | 200km | 400km | 600km | 800km | 1000km | 1200km |

1 cm on the map = 200 km on the ground

| 0 | 200miles | 400miles | 600miles | 800miles |

1 inch on the map = 320 miles on the ground

This box
shows
the scale
of the map. The scale is written in different ways.
The map is drawn to a scale of 1:20,000,000, which
means that the distance between two places on the
ground is exactly 20 million times bigger than it is
on this page! Other maps in this atlas are drawn to
different scales: little Belgium (page 24) is drawn at
a scale of 1:2 million, while the largest country in
the world is drawn at a scale of 1:45 million (Russia,
page 40). Another way of writing the scale of this
map is to say that 1 centimetre on the map is equal
to 200 kilometres on the ground in West Africa.
And this is how the scale line is drawn.

You can use the scale line to make your own scale
ruler. Put the straight edge of a strip of paper against
the scale line and mark the position of 200, 400,
600 kilometres, etc. (Or use the scale in miles if you
prefer.) Carefully number each mark. Now move
your scale ruler over the map to see how far it is
between places. For example, Accra to Abidjan is
400 kilometres.

Height of the land

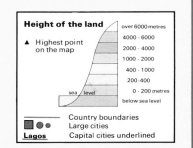

The countries of West
Africa are coloured so that
you can tell the height of
the land. Green shows the
lowest land. Often the real
land will not look green – in the dry season the grass is
brown. The higher land is coloured yellow or brown,
even though some parts are covered with thick green
forest! The highest point in West Africa is shown with
a small black triangle – find it in square C2 – but the
mountains are not high enough to be shown in mauve
or white: look for these on page 44. And to find land
below sea-level, try page 24. Cameroon has some
dramatic mountains (see page 57), but elsewhere the
change from lowland to highland is often quite gentle.
The 'shadows' on the map help you to see which
mountains have steep slopes.

Water features are shown in blue, and their names
are in *italic print*. These include the sea, big rivers and
lakes, such as *Lake Chad* (D1) and *Lake Volta* (B2).
Blue dashes show rivers which dry up for some of
the year.

EUROPE

The map shows the great North European plain that stretches from the Atlantic Ocean to Russia. This plain has most of Europe's best farmland, and many of the biggest cities. To the north of the plain are the snowy mountains of Scandinavia. To the south are even higher mountains: the Pyrenees, the Alps and Carpathians, and the Caucasus Mountains.

Southern Europe has hills and mountains by the Mediterranean Sea. The small areas of lowland are carefully farmed.

Puzzle picture

Western Europe's most important building.
★ What building is it?
★ Where is it?
★ Why does it look so strange?
(Answers on page 96.)

► These twelve car-plates are from the twelve countries of the European Community (Common Market). Can you name them?

(Answers on page 96.)

COPYRIGHT. GEORGE PHILIP & SON LTD.

▼ *Germany/Austria border.* There are many contrasts in Europe. This photograph shows farmland (foreground); woodland (centre); and mountains (the Alps, in the background); find the Alps on the map on page 18. Another important contrast is not visible. The foreground is in Germany, a big country; the background is in Austria, a small country.

Fact box: Europe

Area 10,531,000 square kilometres (including European Russia)

Highest point Mt Elbrus (Russia), 5633 metres

Lowest point Shores of Caspian Sea, 38 metres below sea-level

Longest river Volga (Russia), 3690 kilometres

Largest lake Caspian Sea★, 360,700 square kilometres

Biggest country Russia★, 17,075,000 square kilometres (total area)

Smallest country Vatican City★ (in Rome, Italy), less than half a square kilometre

Richest country Switzerland

Poorest country Albania

Most crowded country Malta

Least crowded country Iceland

★A *world record* as well as a European record

The countries of Georgia, Armenia and Azerbaijan are really in Asia but are also included on this map and on page 36 because they are at a larger scale.

BRITISH ISLES

Scale 1:5 000 000

0   50km   100km   150km   200km   250km

1 cm on the map = 50 km on the ground

0   50miles   100miles   150miles

1 inch on the map = 80 miles on the ground

Height of the land

- over 6000 metres
- 4000 - 6000
- 2000 - 4000
- 1000 - 2000
- 400 - 1000
- 200 - 400
- 0 - 200 metres

sea level

below sea level

▲ Highest point on the map

Country boundaries
Large cities
London Capital cities underlined

Orkney Islands

Shetland Islands

Wick

Hebrides

Lewis

Skye

Inverness

North West Highlands

Ben Nevis 1343 ▲

Grampians

Mull

SCOTLAND

Dundee

Oban

Perth

Aberdeen

Islay

Firth of Forth

Glasgow ■   ■ **Edinburgh**

Arran

ATLANTIC

OCEAN

Southern Uplands

Londonderry

NORTHERN

L. Neagh

Belfast

IRELAND

Armagh

Achill Sound

Newcastle

Carlisle

Sunderland

Middlesbrough

Isle of Man

Douglas

IRELAND

Irish Sea

Galway   Athlone

Dublin

Shannon

Holyhead

Anglesey

York

Bradford

Leeds   Hull

Manchester

Liverpool

Sheffield

UNITED

KINGDOM

North

Sea

P e n n i n e s

Stoke-on-Trent   Derby   Nottingham

Wicklow Mts.

Wexford

Waterford

Snowdon 1085 ▲

Cambrian Mountains

W A L E S

Aberystwyth

Trent

The Wash

E N G L A N D

Birmingham ■

Coventry

Worcester

Northampton

Cambridge

Ipswich

Norwich

Cork

Saint George's Channel

Severn

Avon

Wye

Gloucester

Luton

Oxford

NETHERLANDS

Swansea

Port Talbot

Cardiff

Bristol

Cotswolds

Thames

London ■

Reading

Canterbury

Dover

Bristol Channel

Southampton

Brighton

Strait of Dover

BELGIUM

Exeter

Bournemouth

Portsmouth

Isle of Wight

Plymouth

Land's End   Penzance

Isles of Scilly

English Channel

FRANCE

West from Greenwich   0°   East from Greenwich

COPYRIGHT GEORGE PHILIP & SON LTD

The Highlands of Scotland are very beautiful. The hard rocks are hundreds of millions of years old, and they were eroded by glaciers in the Ice Age.

Often, clouds cover the mountains, and there is a lot of rain. It is hard to make a living here.

What do the flags mean?

▼ The Union Jack is made from three flags: the red-on-white cross (+) of St George (England); the white-on-blue cross (×) of St Andrew (Scotland); and the red-on-white cross (×) of St Patrick (Ireland) – although most of Ireland is independent! St David (Wales) is not included, even though Wales is part of the UK.

▼ The Republic of Ireland flag shows a white stripe (for peace) between orange (Protestants) and green (Roman Catholics).

▲ **Industry in South Wales.** *This big chemical works is at Port Talbot, between Swansea and Cardiff. The big towers are cooling towers. The tall chimney on the right is part of the power station for the site. You can see sand-dunes in the foreground.*

▲ *The Cotswolds, England, are limestone hills. A little village built long ago from the limestone rock nestles at the foot of the hill, where a spring gives pure water. Woodland, grassland and ploughed land still cover much of England.*

The United Kingdom is made up of Great Britain (England, Scotland and Wales) and Northern Ireland. The UK was the most important country in the world 150 years ago. Many old factories and coal mines have now closed down, and several million people now have no jobs. Unemployment is worst in the north. Much of the UK is still quiet and beautiful (see photograph above).

The Republic of Ireland is a completely separate country from the UK. There were twice as many people in Ireland 150 years ago as there are today. In the west, many abandoned farms can be seen. Farming is still important, and Irish butter and cream are famous. New factories have been built in many towns. Even so, many Irish people have moved to the UK or to the USA to find work.

Can you spot eight famous London landmarks on this stamp? (Answer on page 96.)

▼ *Ireland: harvesting reeds in the far west, near Achill Sound. Traditional scenes like this can sometimes still be seen.*

SCANDINAVIA

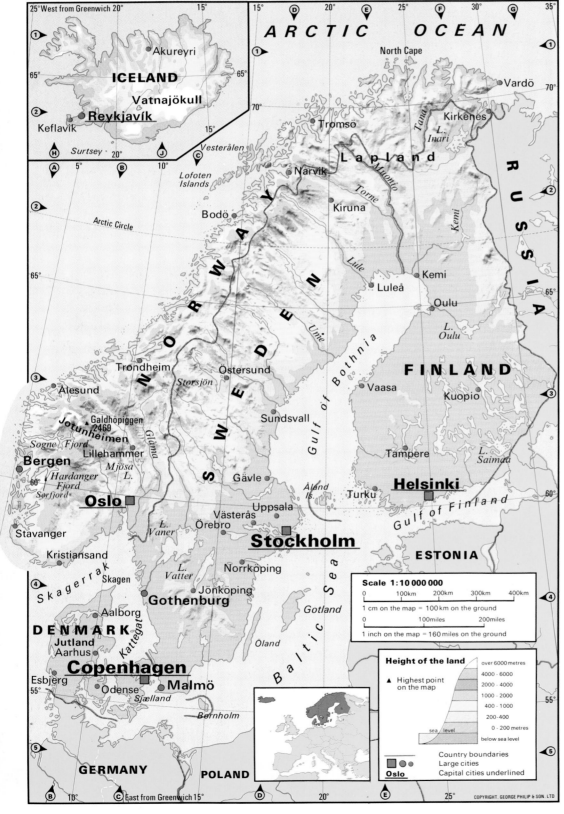

Map labels (clockwise / by region):

25° West from Greenwich 20° 15° 15° 20° 25° 30° 35°

ARCTIC OCEAN

North Cape

ICELAND
Akureyri
65°
Vatnajökull
Reykjavík
Keflavík
Surtsey 20° Vesterålen

Vardö
70°
Kirkenes
L. Inari
Tromsö
Lapland
Narvik
Torne
Kiruna
Bodö
Arctic Circle
Lofoten Islands
Lule
Kemi
Luleå
Oulu
L. Oulu
Trondheim
Östersund
FINLAND
Ålesund
Storsjön
Vaasa
Kuopio
Galdhöpiggen 2469
Jotunheimen
Glåma
Sundsvall
Sogne Fjord
Lillehammer
Bergen
Mjösa L.
Gävle
L. Saimaa
Hardanger Fjord
Tampere
Sörfjord
Oslo
Åland Is.
Helsinki
Stavanger
Västerås
Uppsala
Turku
Gulf of Finland
L. Vaner
Örebro
Stockholm
Kristiansand
Norrköping
ESTONIA
Skagerrak
Skagen
L. Vatter
Jönköping
Gotland
Gothenburg
Aalborg
Öland
DENMARK
Jutland
Kattegat
Aarhus
Copenhagen
Esbjerg
Odense
Malmö
Sjælland
Bornholm
GERMANY
POLAND
Baltic Sea

N O R W A Y   S W E D E N   R U S S I A

Scale 1:10 000 000

| 0 | 100km | 200km | 300km | 400km |

1 cm on the map = 100 km on the ground

| 0 | 100miles | 200miles |

1 inch on the map = 160 miles on the ground

Height of the land

	over 6000 metres
▲ Highest point on the map	4000 - 6000
	2000 - 4000
	1000 - 2000
	400 - 1000
	200 - 400
	0 - 200 metres
sea level	below sea level

Country boundaries
Large cities
Oslo Capital cities underlined

COPYRIGHT. GEORGE PHILIP & SON. LTD

B 10° C East from Greenwich 15° D 20° E 25°

Land of ice and fire

Iceland has many volcanoes.

▼ Most are quiet and peaceful.

EUROPA CEPT
ÍSLAND 85

JARÐELDAR Á HEIMAEY 1973
ÍSLAND 25

But... sometimes a great volcanic ▲ eruption lights up the night sky and the light is reflected in the sea.

Only 250,000 people live in Iceland. It is near the Arctic Circle and there is ice on the mountains, in glaciers and ice-sheets.
   The sea stays ice-free and is full of fish. Iceland has an important fishing fleet.

▲ *Sørfjord is a branch of Hardanger Fjord on the west coast of Norway. A fjord is a long, narrow, deep inlet of the sea with steep sides. Fjords were dug by valley glaciers in the Ice Age. Try to spot a red car: it shows you how steep and high the fjord sides are. The road is cut into solid rock.*

▲ **Forests and lakes in Finland.**
*Most of southern Finland is forested.
The ice-sheets scraped hollows in the
rocks and there are lots of beautiful
lakes. The trees are cut down for
timber, woodpulp, paper, chipboard,
matches and other products that are
sold abroad.*

The mountains of Norway and
Iceland are high and rugged. There
are ice-sheets and glaciers even today.
You can see snow on the highest land
in the photograph of the fjord.
   Southern Sweden and all of
Denmark are lowland. This land was
formed from sand and gravel brought
by ice-sheets in the Ice Age. The
sandy parts do not have good soil,

▶ **Gothenburg** *is the main port on
the west coast of Sweden. The sea
does not freeze here for long.*

▼ **Legoland** *is a model village
beside the Lego factory in Denmark.
Everything is made of Lego! This is
a model of a fishing village in the
Lofoten Islands of Norway.*

but the clay lands grow very good
crops.
   The five countries of Scandinavia
have small populations. Most people
live in towns and cities, and hardly
anyone is poor. Lapland, in the far
north, is beyond the Arctic Circle.
Very few people live here.

▲ **Reindeer in Lapland.** *Lapland
is the northern part of Norway,
Sweden and Finland, where the
Lapps live. They keep reindeer for
their milk, meat and leather, and
also to pull sledges. Notice the
warm and colourful clothes the
Lapps wear.*

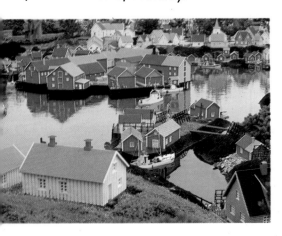

BENELUX

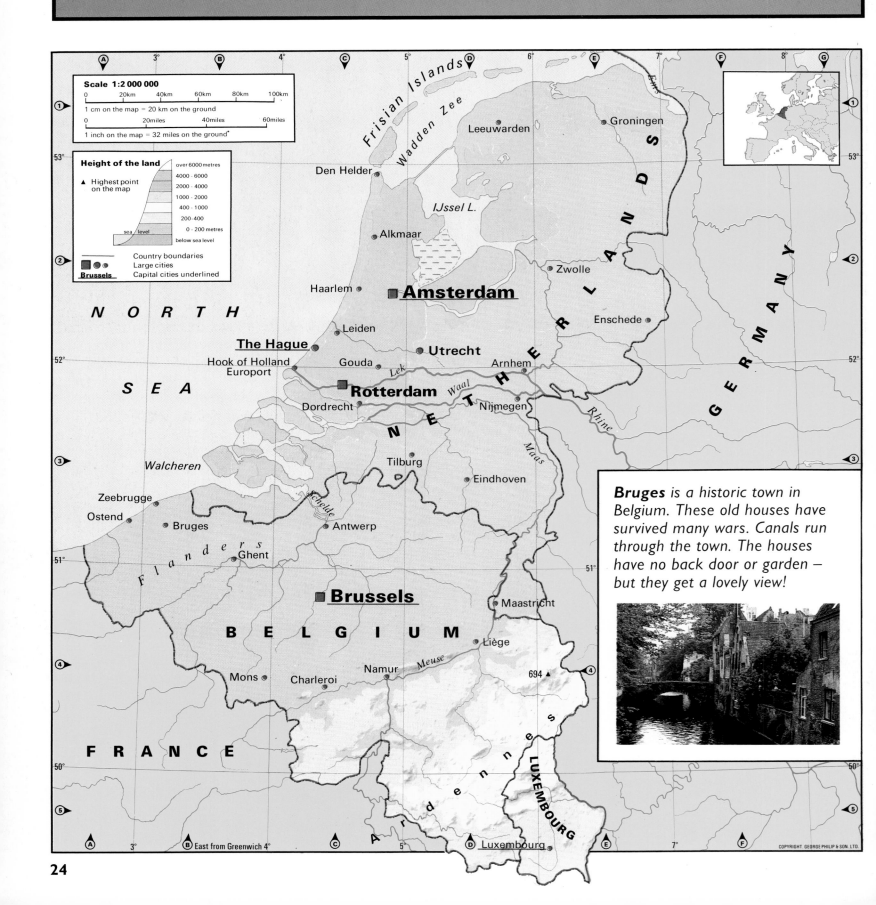

Scale 1:2 000 000

0   20km   40km   60km   80km   100km

1 cm on the map = 20 km on the ground

0   20miles   40miles   60miles

1 inch on the map = 32 miles on the ground*

Height of the land

	over 6000 metres
▲ Highest point on the map	4000 - 6000
	2000 - 4000
	1000 - 2000
	400 - 1000
	200 - 400
sea level	0 - 200 metres
	below sea level

━━━ Country boundaries
■ ● ● Large cities
Brussels Capital cities underlined

Frisian Islands

Wadden Zee

Leeuwarden

Groningen

Den Helder

IJssel L.

Alkmaar

Zwolle

Haarlem

■ **Amsterdam**

Enschede

N E T H E R L A N D S

G E R M A N Y

Leiden

The Hague

Utrecht

Hook of Holland
Europort

Gouda

Lek

Arnhem

Rotterdam

Waal

Dordrecht

Nijmegen

Rhine

N O R T H

S E A

Walcheren

Maas

Tilburg

Eindhoven

Zeebrugge

Schelde

Ostend

Bruges

Antwerp

F l a n d e r s

Ghent

■ **Brussels**

Maastricht

B E L G I U M

Liège

Namur

Meuse

694 ▲

Mons

Charleroi

A r d e n n e s

F R A N C E

L U X E M B O U R G

Luxembourg

Bruges *is a historic town in Belgium. These old houses have survived many wars. Canals run through the town. The houses have no back door or garden – but they get a lovely view!*

COPYRIGHT GEORGE PHILIP & SON. LTD.

East from Greenwich 4°

Spot the difference

What is the difference between these two coins from Belgium? And why is there a difference? (Answer on page 96.)

▼ *Europort, Rotterdam.*
Rotterdam is by far the biggest port in the whole world: only a few of the docks can be seen here. Ships come from all over the world, and barges travel along the River Rhine and the canals of Europe to reach the port.

Benelux is a word made up from **Be**lgium, **Ne**therlands and **Lux**embourg. Fortunately, the first two letters of each name are the same in most languages, so everyone can understand the word. These three countries agreed to co-operate soon after World War 2. But they still have their very own KING (of Belgium), QUEEN (of the Netherlands) and GRAND DUKE (of Luxembourg).

The Benelux countries are all small and are the most crowded in mainland Europe, but there is plenty of countryside too. Most of the land is low and flat, so they are sometimes called the Low Countries. But Luxembourg and eastern Belgium have pleasant wooded hills called the Ardennes. There are lots of modern industries, but the coalfield of central Belgium is a problem area because most of the coal mines have closed.

▲ *Gouda market. See the clogs for sale among the wellingtons and wheelbarrows! Clogs are worn by some farmers and market gardeners, but many people prefer boots for working on the marshy land.*

Are these windmills?

No, these are *not* windmills! They are really wind-*pumps*. They were used to pump water *up* from the fields into rivers and canals. The river is higher than the land! Much of the Netherlands was drained for farmland in this way. Nowadays, powerful diesel or electric pumps are used instead.

FRANCE

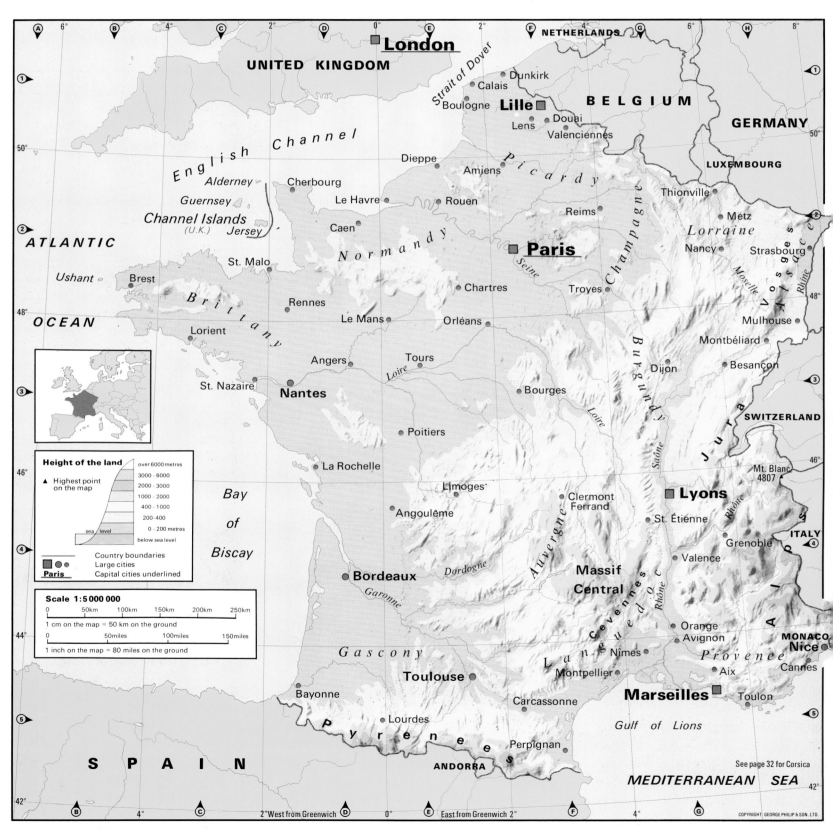

United Kingdom — London

Netherlands

Belgium

Germany

Dunkirk · Calais · Boulogne · **Lille** · Lens · Douai · Valenciennes

Luxembourg

Dieppe · Amiens · *Picardy* · Thionville · Metz

English Channel

Alderney · Guernsey · Channel Islands (U.K.) · Jersey · Cherbourg · Le Havre · Rouen · Reims · *Lorraine* · Nancy · Strasbourg

Normandy · Caen · **Paris** · *Champagne* · Troyes · *Seine* · Mulhouse · Montbéliard · Besançon

Ushant · Brest · St. Malo · *Brittany* · Rennes · Chartres · Le Mans · Orléans · *Burgundy* · Dijon

Atlantic Ocean · Lorient · Angers · Tours · *Loire* · Bourges · *Saône* · **Switzerland**

St. Nazaire · **Nantes** · Poitiers · Mt. Blanc 4807 · *Jura*

La Rochelle · Limoges · Clermont Ferrand · **Lyons** · *Rhône* · St. Étienne · Grenoble · **Italy**

Angoulême · *Auvergne* · Valence · *Alps*

Bay of Biscay · **Bordeaux** · *Garonne* · *Dordogne* · **Massif Central** · *Cévennes* · Orange · Avignon · **Monaco** · **Nice** · Cannes

Gascony · *Languedoc* · *Rhône* · Nîmes · Aix · *Provence*

Toulouse · Bayonne · Montpellier · **Marseilles** · Toulon

Carcassonne · Lourdes · *Pyrenees* · Perpignan · *Gulf of Lions*

Spain · Andorra · **Mediterranean Sea**

See page 32 for Corsica

Height of the land

▲ Highest point on the map

over 6000 metres
3000 – 6000
2000 – 3000
1000 – 2000
400 – 1000
200 – 400
sea level 0 – 200 metres
below sea level

■ ● ● Country boundaries / Large cities
Paris Capital cities underlined

Scale 1:5 000 000

0 50km 100km 150km 200km 250km
1 cm on the map = 50 km on the ground

0 50miles 100miles 150miles
1 inch on the map = 80 miles on the ground

French wine

A label from a bottle of French wine. The vines are growing in long straight rows on both sides of the valley. More wine is drunk in France than in any other country.

 Market at Nice. Which vegetables can you recognize on this stall? (Answer on page 96.) Every town in France has a good market. Housewives choose fresh fruit and vegetables very carefully.

France is a country with three coastlines: can you see which these are? It is hot in summer in the south, but it is usually cool in the mountains and in the north. France is the biggest country in Western Europe, so there are big contrasts between north and south.

The highest mountains are the Alps in the south-east and the Pyrenees in the south-west. They are popular for skiing in winter and for summer holidays too. More than half the country is lowland, and farming is very important. Besides fruit, vegetables and wine, France is famous for its many different cheeses.

France is changing fast. The number of people living in villages is going down, and the population of the cities is growing – partly swelled by Arabs from North Africa who have come to live in France. The biggest city is Paris, which is also the capital. Ten million people now live in the Paris region, and five big new towns have been built around Paris.

▼ *Mont Blanc.* The 'White Mountain' is the highest mountain in Western Europe. It is 4807 metres high. Even in summer (as here) it is covered in snow. Cable-cars take tourists and skiers up the mountain.

Made in France

▲ These *Majorette* models are made in France. They include a Renault van, a Michelin lorry, an Air France bus and a Paris bus. The most popular French cars are:

Renault   Citroën   Peugeot

What else can you find that is made in France? In our home we have:

BIC ball-point pens
a LE CREUSET frying-pan
ARCOROC glassware
ARCOPOL cups and saucers
a MOULINEX mixer
and a PHILIPS washing machine

GERMANY AND AUSTRIA

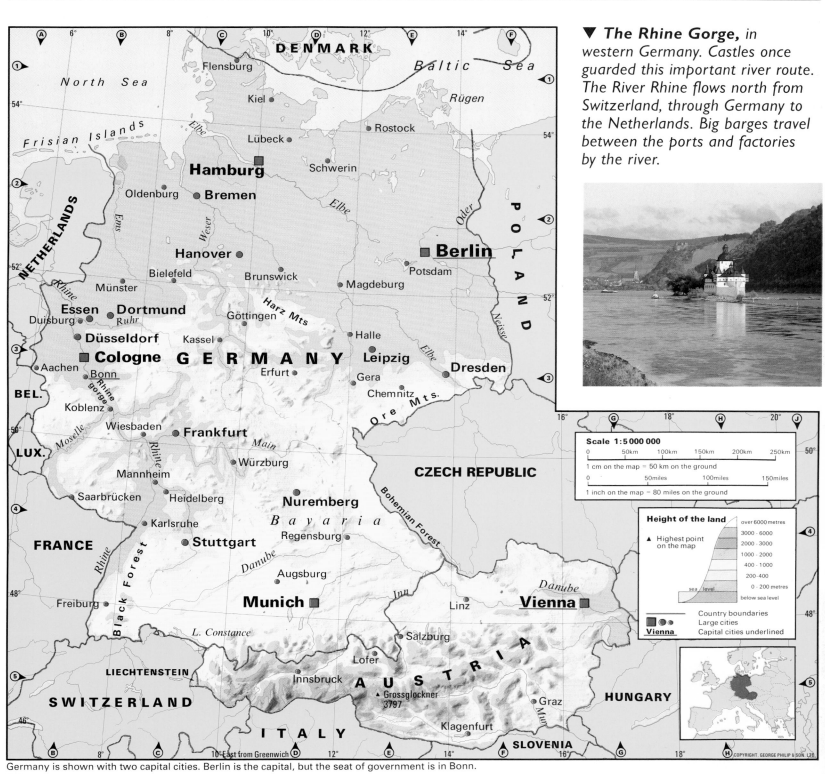

▼ The Rhine Gorge, in western Germany. Castles once guarded this important river route. The River Rhine flows north from Switzerland, through Germany to the Netherlands. Big barges travel between the ports and factories by the river.

DENMARK

Baltic Sea

North Sea

Flensburg

Kiel

Rügen

Lübeck

Rostock

Frisian Islands

Schwerin

Hamburg

NETHERLANDS

Oldenburg

Bremen

Elbe

Ems

Weser

Oder

P O L A N D

Hanover

Bielefeld

Brunswick

■ **Berlin**

Potsdam

Münster

Magdeburg

Essen **Dortmund**

Harz Mts

Göttingen

Neisse

Duisburg

Ruhr

Düsseldorf

Kassel

Halle

Cologne

G E R M A N Y

Leipzig

Aachen

Bonn

Erfurt

Gera

Elbe

Dresden

BEL.

Rhine gorge

Chemnitz

Ore Mts.

Koblenz

Wiesbaden

Frankfurt

Main

CZECH REPUBLIC

LUX.

Moselle

Rhine

Würzburg

Mannheim

Saarbrücken

Heidelberg

Nuremberg

Bohemian Forest

FRANCE

B a v a r i a

Karlsruhe

Regensburg

Black Forest

Stuttgart

Danube

Augsburg

Danube

Inn

Freiburg

Munich ■

Linz

Vienna ■

L. Constance

Salzburg

Lofer

A U S T R I A

LIECHTENSTEIN

Innsbruck

▲ Grossglockner

Graz

HUNGARY

3797

SWITZERLAND

Klagenfurt

Mun

I T A L Y

SLOVENIA

10°East from Greenwich

Scale 1:5 000 000

0   50km   100km   150km   200km   250km

1 cm on the map = 50 km on the ground

0   50miles   100miles   150miles

1 inch on the map = 80 miles on the ground

Height of the land

over 6000 metres
3000 - 6000
2000 - 3000
1000 - 2000
400 - 1000
200 - 400
0 - 200 metres
below sea level

▲ Highest point on the map

sea level

Country boundaries
Large cities
Vienna   Capital cities underlined

COPYRIGHT. GEORGE PHILIP & SON. LTD

Germany is shown with two capital cities. Berlin is the capital, but the seat of government is in Bonn.

Germany has more people than any other European country apart from Russia. Most of the 80 million Germans live in towns and cities. Several million people called 'guest workers' have come from southern Europe and Turkey to work in Germany's factories. But nowadays there is unemployment in Germany, as in other European countries, and many 'guest workers' have returned home. Among the many different goods made in Germany there are excellent cars: BMW, Ford, Mercedes, Opel, Porsche and Volkswagen.

There is also plenty of beautiful uncrowded countryside. The north is mostly lowland. Parts of the south, such as the Black Forest, are mountainous and popular for holidays.

▲ *Sausages, beer and pretzels are popular in Germany. The beer from Munich is made from barley; the pretzels (dry biscuits) are made from wheat; the big sausages are made from pork.*

Transport stamps

Germany has excellent railways. The stamps show two clever answers to the problems of overcrowding: a double-deck passenger train, and a monorail. The train hangs from the one rail, which is built over the River Wupper to save space. This is near the River Ruhr.

▼ *The Alps are popular for winter sports. This guesthouse in the village of Lofer, Austria, is full of skiers in winter. Trees cover the lower slopes of the mountains: the skiers will go up to the snow-slopes above the trees.*

Austria. Until 1918, Austria and Hungary were linked, and ruled a great Empire which included much of Central Europe and Slovenia, Croatia and Bosnia (see page 34). But now Austria is a small, peaceful country.

In the west of Austria are the high Alps, and many tourists come to enjoy the beautiful scenery and winter sports. Busy motorways and electric railways cross the Austrian Alps to link Germany with Italy.

Most Austrians live in the lower eastern part of the country. The capital is Vienna on the River Danube. It was once near the centre of the Austrian Empire; now it is in a corner of the country.

Germany was one country from 1870 to 1945. In 1990 it became one country again. From 1945 until 1990, it was divided into West Germany and East Germany, and there was a border fence between the two, with armed guards. To end World War 2 in 1945, Germany was invaded from west and east at the same time. The area occupied by the USSR forces became East Germany, with a Communist government. The rest of Germany was called West Germany, even though it included southern Germany too! Now, all Germany is one country again. But its area is still smaller than it was before 1945, because all the land east of the Rivers Oder and Neisse is now in Poland.

Berlin is the capital and the biggest city of Germany. From 1945 until 1990 it was divided into two. East Berlin was the capital of East Germany, but West Berlin was still part of West Germany – even though it was surrounded by East Germany. The Berlin Wall divided the city; it was knocked down in 1989.

▲ *The international clock in Berlin, which tells the time of the whole world! It is 16.00 hours (4 pm) in Berlin: what time is it in Reykjavik (Iceland) and in Helsinki (Finland)? And how does the clock work? (Answers on page 96.)*

SPAIN AND PORTUGAL

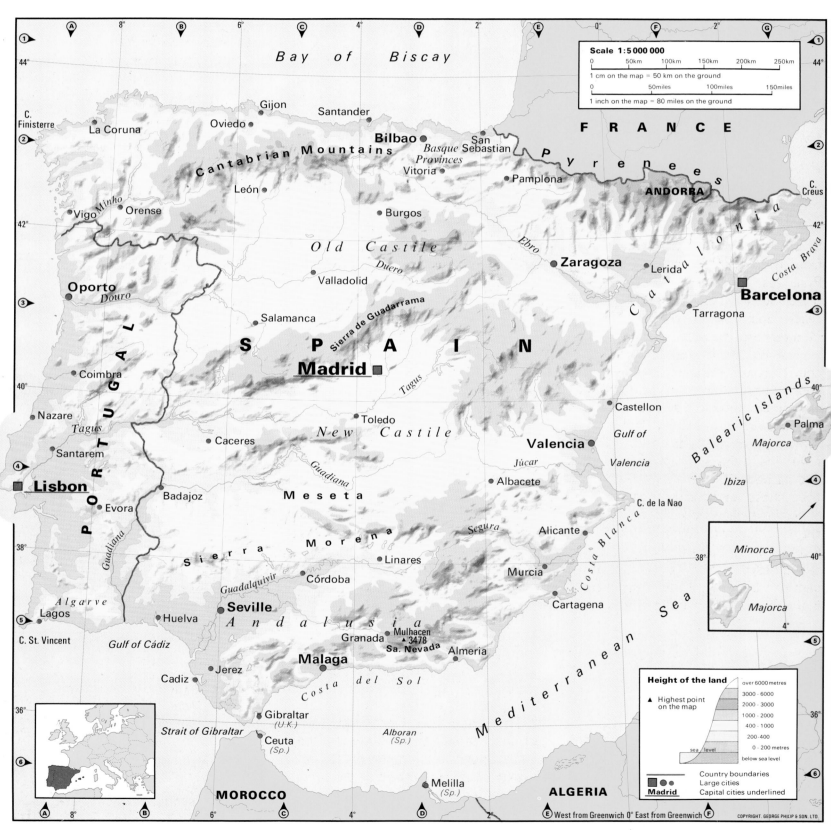

Scale 1:5 000 000

| 0 | 50km | 100km | 150km | 200km | 250km |

1 cm on the map = 50 km on the ground

| 0 | 50miles | 100miles | 150miles |

1 inch on the map = 80 miles on the ground

Bay of Biscay

FRANCE

C. Finisterre
La Coruna
Gijon
Santander
Oviedo
Bilbao
San Sebastian
Basque Provinces
Vitoria
Pamplona
Pyrenees
ANDORRA
C. Creus

Cantabrian Mountains
León
Burgos

Vigo
Minho
Orense
Old Castile
Duero
Zaragoza
Lerida
Catalonia
Costa Brava

Oporto
Douro
Valladolid
Barcelona
Tarragona

Salamanca
Sierra de Guadarrama
S P A I N

Madrid
Tagus

Coimbra
Castellon
Balearic Islands
Palma

P O R T U G A L
Nazare
Tagus
Caceres
New Castile
Valencia
Gulf of Valencia
Majorca
Santarem
Júcar
Ibiza

Lisbon
Badajoz
Guadiana
Meseta
Albacete
C. de la Nao

Evora
Guadiana
Segura
Alicante
Costa Blanca

Sierra Morena
Linares
Murcia
Minorca

Algarve
Córdoba
Cartagena
Majorca
Lagos
Guadalquivir
Seville
Huelva
Andalusia
C. St. Vincent
Gulf of Cádiz
Granada *Mulhacen*
▲ 3478
Sa. Nevada
Almeria

Cadiz
Jerez
Malaga
Costa del Sol
Mediterranean Sea

Gibraltar (U.K.)
Strait of Gibraltar
Ceuta (Sp.)
Alboran (Sp.)

Melilla (Sp.)
MOROCCO
ALGERIA

West from Greenwich 0° East from Greenwich

COPYRIGHT. GEORGE PHILIP & SON. LTD.

Height of the land

	over 6000 metres
	3000 - 6000
	2000 - 3000
	1000 - 2000
	400 - 1000
	200 - 400
	0 - 200 metres
sea level	below sea level

▲ Highest point on the map

Country boundaries
■ ● ● Large cities
Madrid Capital cities underlined

◀ **Village in southern Spain.** The old houses crowd closely together, and roads are very narrow: wide enough for a donkey, but not for lorries. People whitewash their houses to reflect the rays of the hot sun. Olive trees grow on the hills.

Did you know?

Gibraltar is still a British colony, but it is only 6 square kilometres in area. Spain still owns two towns in Morocco: *Ceuta* and *Melilla*. Spain wants Gibraltar – and Morocco wants Ceuta and Melilla. The arguments continue . . . .

Spain and Portugal are separated from the rest of Europe by the high Pyrenees Mountains. Most people travelling by land from the north reach Spain along the Atlantic or Mediterranean coasts.

The Meseta is the high plateau of central Spain. Winters are very cold, and summers are very hot. Olives and vines are the main crops. But cars are the biggest export from Spain nowadays. Both Spain and Portugal have fine cities with great churches and cathedrals, built when they were the richest countries in the world.

Spain is very popular for holidays: the Costa Brava (Rugged Coast), the Costa del Sol (Coast of the Sun), and the Balearic Islands are crowded in summer. In Portugal the Algarve coast is the most popular holiday area.

▼ **The Alhambra Palace, Granada.** This beautiful palace was built by the Moors (Arabs from North Africa). The Moors ruled southern Spain for hundreds of years, until 1492. The Arabs brought new crops and new ideas to Europe.

Spanish coins

Spain became a monarchy again in 1975; the coin shows King Juan Carlos I.

In 1982, the World Cup was held in Spain: this special coin shows a football and the world.

▼ **Bull-ring and flats, Malaga.** The bull-ring is a big and important building in Spanish cities. High blocks of flats are typical of modern Spain. In the background is the blue Mediterranean Sea. Malaga is a large port in southern Spain.

◀ **Sun-dried fish, Portugal.** Sardines caught in the Atlantic Ocean are dried in the strong sunshine at Nazare, Portugal. Many of the older ladies wear black clothes, even in summer.

SWITZERLAND AND ITALY

Labels from food
exported from Italy: try making a collection yourself!

▶ **Sorano,** *central Italy. Long ago the hill town was a safe place to live. The houses huddled closely around the castle and the church. Nowadays, a hill town needs a zigzag road to reach it.*

Italy is shaped like a boot: its toe seems to be kicking Sicily! The shape is caused by the long range of fold mountains called the Apennines. The great Roman Empire was centred on Italy, and there are many Roman ruins. Yet Italy was only united as a country less than 150 years ago. Italy has lots of big factories. The Fiat car plant in Turin is one of the largest and most modern in the world.

Swiss record breakers

Switzerland holds some amazing world records.

*The *longest* road tunnel is the St Gotthard tunnel (16.32 kilometres).
*The *longest* stairway is beside the Niesenbahn mountain railway, near Spiez. It has 11,674 steps!
*The *steepest* railway goes up Mount Pilatus. It has a gradient of 48%.

*And Switzerland has been at peace with everyone since 1815. That's quite a record!

Switzerland also has the *oddest* car-plates: CH is from the Latin name for Switzerland:

CH

Confederatio Helvetica.

In **Switzerland** most people live in cities north of the Alps. Switzerland is one of the world's richest countries, with modern banks, offices and factories.

Rivers, dams and waterfalls in the Alps are used for making hydro-electric power: trains, factories and homes in Switzerland all run on cheap electricity. Cable-cars powered by electricity take skiers and tourists high into the beautiful mountains.

▲ **Venice,** *north-east Italy. Travel is by boat, or on foot: there are no cars, because the 'roads' are canals.*

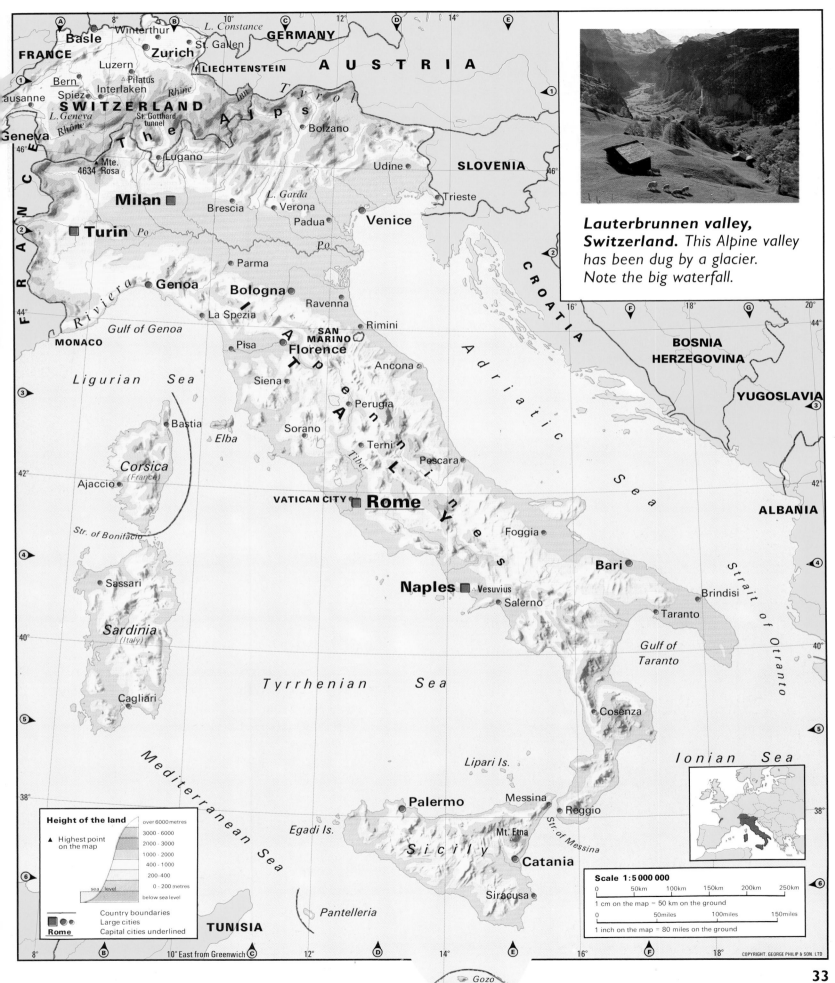

FRANCE

Basle
Winterthur
Zurich
GERMANY
St. Gallen
LIECHTENSTEIN
AUSTRIA
Luzern
Pilatus
Bern
Interlaken
Spiez
SWITZERLAND
Rhine
Inn
Tyrol
L. Constance
Lausanne
L. Geneva
Rhône
St. Gotthard
tunnel
The
Alps
Bolzano
Geneva
Mte.
Rosa
4634
Lugano
Udine
SLOVENIA
Trieste
Milan
Brescia
Verona
L. Garda
Padua
Venice
Turin
Po
Po
Parma
CROATIA
Genoa
Bologna
Ravenna
La Spezia
Rimini
Riviera
Gulf of Genoa
MONACO
Pisa
SAN
MARINO
Florence
Ancona
Adriatic
BOSNIA
HERZEGOVINA
Ligurian   Sea
Siena
A
p
p
e
n
n
i
Perugia
Bastia
Sorano
Elba
Terni
YUGOSLAVIA
Tiber
Pescara
Sea
Corsica
(France)
n
Ajaccio
VATICAN CITY
Rome
ALBANIA
Str. of Bonifacio
Foggia
e
s
Bari
Sardinia
(Italy)
Sassari
Naples
Vesuvius
Brindisi
Salerno
Taranto
Strait of Otranto
Gulf of
Taranto
Cagliari
Tyrrhenian   Sea
Cosenza
Ionian   Sea
Lipari Is.
Palermo
Messina
Reggio
Mediterranean Sea
Egadi Is.
Str. of Messina
Sicily
Mt. Etna
Catania
TUNISIA
Pantelleria
Siracusa

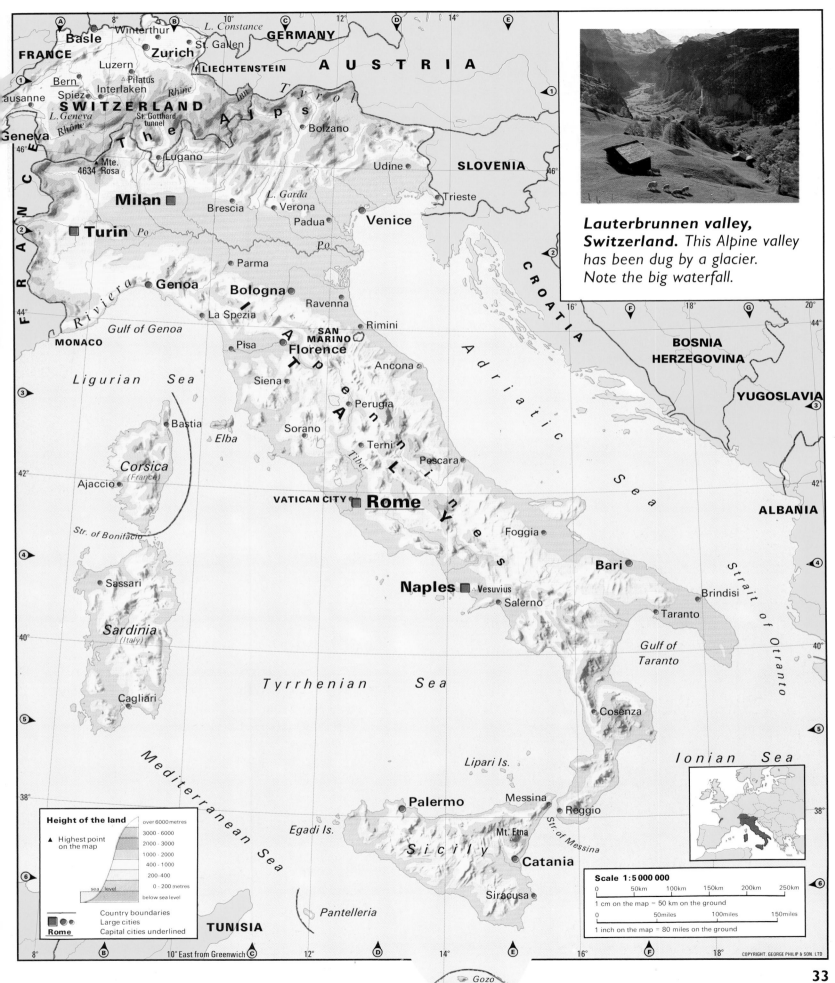
*Lauterbrunnen valley,
Switzerland.* This Alpine valley
has been dug by a glacier.
Note the big waterfall.

Height of the land

▲ Highest point
on the map

over 6000 metres
3000 - 6000
2000 - 3000
1000 - 2000
400 - 1000
200 - 400
0 - 200 metres
below sea level

sea level

▀ ● ● Country boundaries
Large cities
Rome Capital cities underlined

Scale 1:5 000 000

0   50km   100km   150km   200km   250km

1 cm on the map = 50 km on the ground

0   50miles   100miles   150miles

1 inch on the map = 80 miles on the ground

COPYRIGHT: GEORGE PHILIP & SON. LTD

8°   10° East from Greenwich   12°   14°   16°   18°

Gozo
MALTA ● Valletta

SOUTH-EAST EUROPE

Most of south-east Europe is very mountainous, except near the River Danube. Farmers keep sheep and goats in the mountains and grow grain, vines and sunflowers on the lower land.

The coastlines are popular with tourists. There are many holiday resorts beside the Aegean Sea (Greece and Turkey) and the Black Sea (Romania and Bulgaria). The Romanians are building new ski villages in their mountains. All these countries are trying to develop different industries, but this is still one of the poorest parts of Europe.

Albania is the least-known country in all Europe: very few people visit it. No railways crossed the frontier of Albania until 1985.

▲ **Romania.** *Behind the maize (sweetcorn) a huge modern factory brings jobs and money – and pollution too. The tractor and plough on the Romanian coin show that farming is still important. The Romanian language is not hard to understand. Try to read the words on the stamp.*

Yugoslavia was 1 country with 2 alphabets (Latin and Cyrillic), 3 religious groups (Roman Catholic, Orthodox and Muslim), 4 languages and 6 republics. No wonder there were problems! Slovenia, Croatia, Macedonia and Bosnia-Herzegovina have now declared independence.

▲ **Dubrovnik** *is a walled city on the Adriatic coast. It was badly damaged in the Yugoslavian civil war in 1991.*

The Danube

The stamp shows a tourist boat at the gorge on the River Danube called the Iron Gates, on the southern border of Romania. The Danube flows eastwards for 1700 kilometres from Germany to a marshy delta beside the Black Sea. It passes eight countries, and is becoming important for trade. Dams and locks now allow big ships to navigate the river.

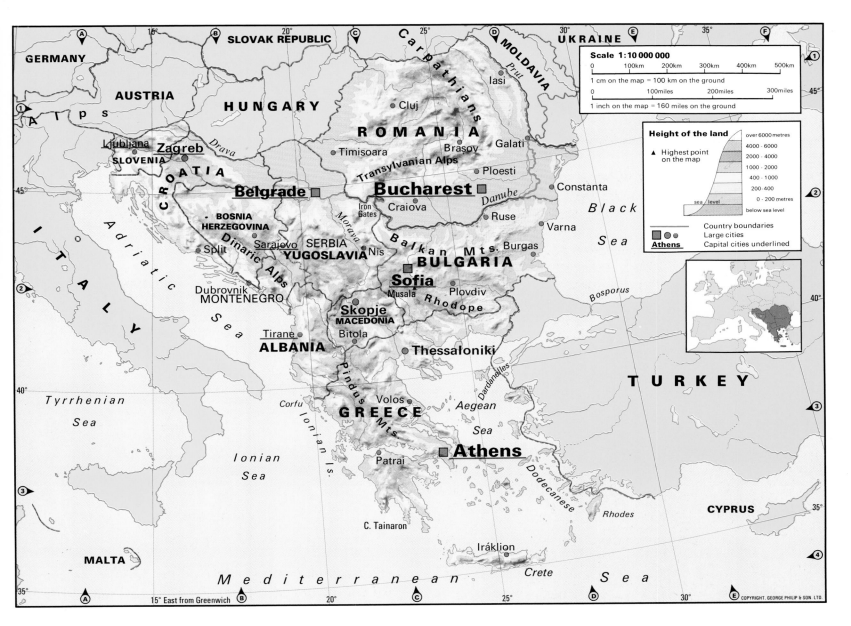

Scale 1:10 000 000

1 cm on the map = 100 km on the ground

1 inch on the map = 160 miles on the ground

Height of the land
- over 6000 metres
- 4000 - 6000
- ▲ Highest point on the map
- 2000 - 4000
- 1000 - 2000
- 400 - 1000
- 200 - 400
- sea level
- 0 - 200 metres
- below sea level

Country boundaries
Large cities
Athens Capital cities underlined

◀ ***Fishing village, Crete.*** *Crete is the biggest of the many islands that form part of **Greece**. The village nestles below the mountains. Some of the fishermen's cottages have become guesthouses for tourists.*

▼ ***The Greek alphabet.*** *The Greeks developed their alphabet before the Romans, and they still use it. Some letters are the same as ours (A, B ...), and some look the same but have a different sound (P, H ...). The other letters are completely different. Some Greek letters appear in the Cyrillic alphabet, which is used in Bulgaria, Yugoslavia and Russia (see page 41). The word alphabet is formed from the first two Greek letters:* alpha *and* beta.

Α	Β	Γ	Δ	Ε	Ζ	Η	Θ	Ι	Κ	Λ	Μ	Ν	Ξ	Ο	Π	Ρ	Σ	Τ	Υ	Φ	Χ	Ψ	Ω
A	V/B	G	D	E	Z	E	TH	I	K	L	M	N	X	O	P	R	S	T	Y	F	CH	PS	O

EASTERN EUROPE

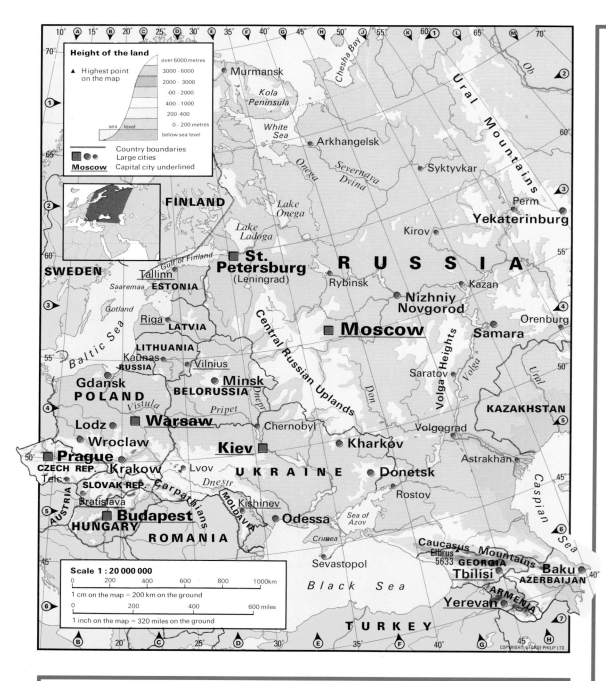

Height of the land

▲ Highest point on the map

over 6000 metres
3000 - 6000
2000 - 3000
·00 - 2000
400 - 1000
200 - 400
0 - 200 metres
below sea level

sea level

☐ ◉ Country boundaries
Large cities
Moscow Capital city underlined

Scale 1 : 20 000 000

0   200   400   600   800   1000km

1 cm on the map = 200 km on the ground

0   200   400   600 miles

1 inch on the map = 320 miles on the ground

COPYRIGHT GEORGE PHILIP LTD.

Three 're-born' countries

In 1991 Estonia, Latvia and Lithuania became independent countries – again. They were also independent from 1918 to 1940. Sometimes these three countries are called 'The Baltic Republics', because they all have a coastline on the Baltic Sea.

▲ This stamp of the new Estonia shows a map of Europe, with the latitude and longitude of Estonia – and an inset map shows the shape of the country. The flag-stamp shows the flag of Estonia, and the name of Estonia in six languages.

► The badge of Estonia has three lions – they are on the map-stamp, and on this old stamp from 1928 as well.

▼ Two of the first stamps of the new Latvia ('Lietuva') show black storks in a forest, and cranes in a wetland area.

A church in a lake!

Europe's longest river is called the Volga. Great dams have been built on this river, so big lakes have formed behind the dams – and whole villages have vanished beneath the water. That is why there is now a church in a lake.

◀ *Ploughing the fields, Poland.* Horses are still used for ploughing fields in many parts of Poland. Look carefully . . . . How many horses are pulling the plough?

Poland has a coastline on the Baltic Sea. There are huge shipbuilding factories at Gdansk. There are big factories in the towns in the south, too, where there is plenty of coal. Most of the country is flat farmland.

Czechoslovakia split into two countries in 1993. The **Czech Republic** is west of the **Slovak Republic**. Both countries have beautiful hills and mountains, with fine pine trees. Skoda cars come from the Czech Republic.

Hungary is a small, flat country. Mostly it is farmland, but Hungary also has the biggest bus factory in the world. Buda and Pest were twin cities, on either side of the River Danube. Now they have become Budapest, the capital city.

Languages. Polish, Czech and Slovak are all Slavic languages. Hungarian is a totally different language; it came from central Asia. You can see some Hungarian words on the stamps and on the boat in the photograph.

▼ *Budapest, Hungary: a vintage paddle steamer on the River Danube is passing the parliament building.*

The seasons in Eastern Europe:

Winter can be very cold in eastern Europe, so cross-country skiing is popular. But summers are warm and sunny. Lake Balaton is a popular holiday area in Hungary.

▲ *Town square in Telc, Czech Republic.* The historic centres of towns are carefully preserved in Eastern Europe. Some have been totally rebuilt in the old style, after wartime bombing.

ASIA

Asia is the world's biggest continent, stretching from the cold Arctic Ocean in the north, to the warm Indian Ocean in the tropical south.

◀ **Himalayan Mountains, Nepal,** *photographed by the famous mountaineer Chris Bonington. The world's ten highest mountains are all in the Himalayas.*

Mainland Asia nearly reaches the Equator in Malaysia. Several Asian islands are on the Equator: Sumatra, Borneo and Sulawesi. In the west, Asia reaches Europe and the Mediterranean Sea, and in the east Asia reaches the Pacific Ocean, and gets close to Australia. In the centre are the high, empty plateaus of Tibet and Mongolia.

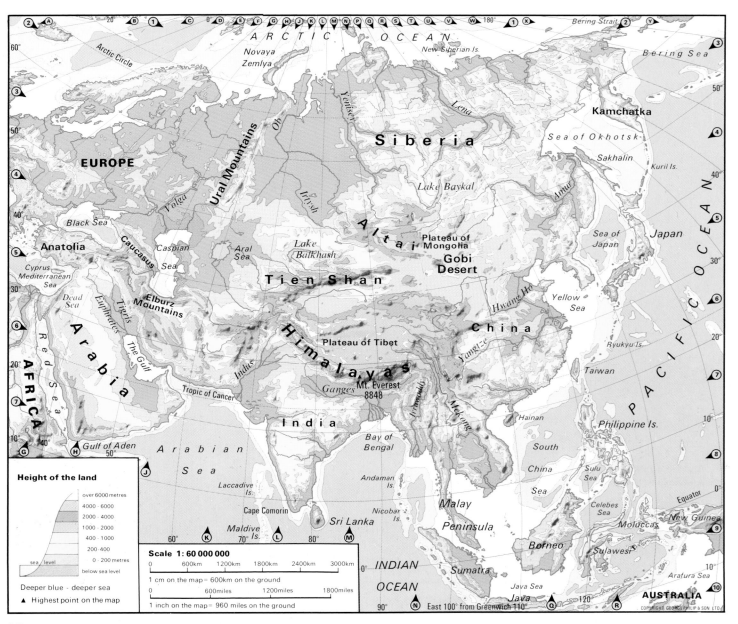

Asian

Afghanistan
Bangladesh
Bhutan
Burma
Cambodia
China
Cyprus
Indonesia
Iran
Israel
Japan
Korea, N & S
Laos
Lebanon
Macao
Maldives
Mongolia
Oman
Philippines
Qatar
Saudi Arabia
Sri Lanka
Syria
Thailand
Turkey
UAE
Vietnam

Height of the land

over 6000 metres
4000 - 6000
2000 - 4000
1000 - 2000
400 - 1000
200 - 400
0 - 200 metres
sea level
below sea level

Deeper blue - deeper sea
▲ Highest point on the map

Scale 1 : 60 000 000

0   600km   1200km   1800km   2400km   3000km

1 cm on the map = 600km on the ground

0   600miles   1200miles   1800miles

1 inch on the map = 960 miles on the ground

Fact box: Asia

Area 44,387,000 square kilometres (including Asiatic Russia)

Highest point Mount Everest★ (Nepal/China), 8848 metres

Lowest point Shores of Dead Sea★ (Israel/Jordan), 400 metres below sea-level

Longest rivers Yenisey (Russia), 5540 kilometres; Yangtze (China), 5530 kilometres

Biggest country Russia★, 17,075,000 square kilometres

Smallest country The Maldives, 298 square kilometres

★A *world record* as well as an Asian record

▶ **Buddhist shrine.** *Religion is very important to most people in Asia. This Buddhist shrine is like many found in Nepal. It has been decorated with prayer flags and painted eyes.*

Two countries cover over half of Asia: Russia and China. India looks quite small – yet it is over ten times as big as Italy or the UK! But some of Asia's important countries are very small indeed, for example Lebanon and Israel in south-west Asia (Middle East); Singapore and Brunei in south-east Asia (Far East).

Over half the world's population lives in Asia. The coastal areas of south and east Asia are the most crowded parts. Seven of the 'top ten' most populated countries in the world are in Asia: China, India, Indonesia, Russia, Japan, Bangladesh and Pakistan (see page 9).

Money

Afghani
Taka
Ngultrum
Kyat
Riel
Yuan
Pound
Rupiah
Rial
Shekel
Yen
Won
Kip
Pound
Pataca
Rufiyaa
Tugrik
Omani
Peso
Riyal
Rial
Rupee
Pound
Baht
Lira
Dirham
Dong

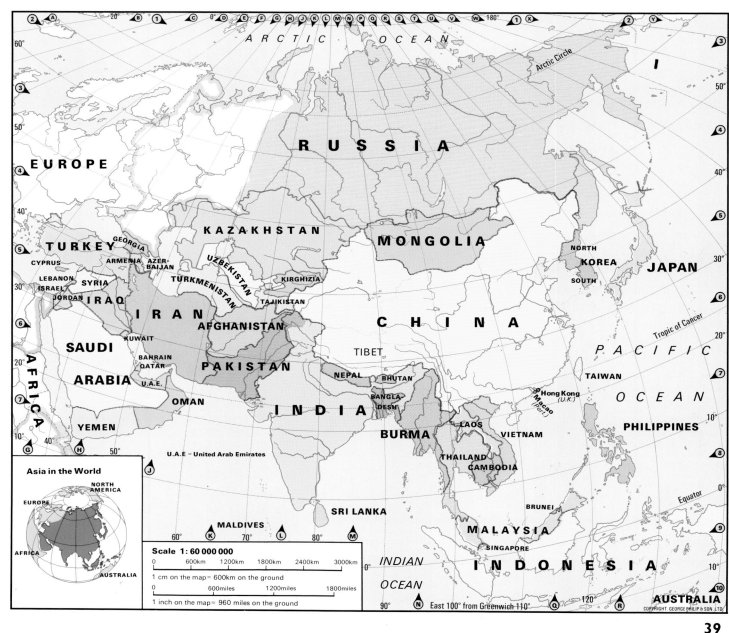

Asia in the World

Scale 1 : 60 000 000

U.A.E = United Arab Emirates

1 cm on the map = 600km on the ground

1 inch on the map = 960 miles on the ground

East 100° from Greenwich

COPYRIGHT GEORGE PHILIP & SON LTD

RUSSIA AND NEIGHBOURS

Scale 1: 45 000 000

1 cm on the map = 450 km on the ground

1 inch on the map = 720 miles on the ground

Height of the land

over 6000 metres	
4000 - 6000	
2000 - 4000	
1000 - 2000	
400 - 1000	
200 - 400	
0 - 200 metres	
below sea level	

▲ Highest point on the map

Country boundaries
Large cities
Moscow Capital city underlined

More details of European Russia are shown on page 36

Understanding the new map

Russia is the biggest country in the world today – even though the USSR split up into 15 republics in 1991.
The other 14 republics make four groups:

3 'Baltic Republics': Estonia, Latvia and Lithuania

3 other European Republics: Belorussia and Ukraine (near Poland); Moldavia (near Romania)

3 small republics south of the Caucasus Mountains (between the Black Sea and the Caspian Sea): Georgia, Armenia and Azerbaijan

5 Central Asian republics: Kazakhstan (the biggest), Uzbekistan, Turkmenistan, Kirghizia and Tajikistan.

Several cities have changed their names back to the pre-Communist name, such as St Petersburg.

▶ **The Siberian steppes.** A horse-cart travels along a track in Siberia. The steppes are not steps! They are part of the world's biggest plain – snow-covered in winter, and with grass or wheat in summer.

Russia stretches across two continents, Europe and Asia. Most people live in the European part, west of the Ural Mountains. But gradually people are moving east to new towns.

Because Russia is so huge, there are many different climates and almost all crops can be grown. The far north is snow-covered for most of the year (see page 89). Further south is the largest forest in the world – a vast area of coniferous trees stretching from the Baltic Sea to the Sea of Okhotsk. Grassy plains, called the steppes, come south of the forest. In some parts, grain is grown on huge farms. Russia also has huge deposits of many different minerals and can supply most of the needs of its many different factories.

The republics of central Asia are mostly in a desert area – hot in summer but bitterly cold in winter. With irrigation, crops such as sugar-cane and cotton grow well.

▲ **The Kremlin, Moscow.**
There are three former churches in the Kremlin; it now houses the government of Russia. The golden domes can be seen far away.

The Cyrillic alphabet

Russian is written in the Cyrillic alphabet. This is partly based on Latin letters (the same as English letters) and partly on Greek letters (see page 35).

The alphabet was invented centuries ago by St Cyril, so that the Russian church could show it was separated from both the Roman and the Greek churches. In Cyrillic, R is written P, and S is written C. So the Metro is written МЕТРО.

Can you understand this message? Use the key below:
Х А Б А Р О В С К(square S4) is on the River А М У Р (see square R3 on the map).

Now can you write Volga (the river) in Russian? Check your answer with a postage stamp on page 36.

▲ **GUM shopping centre, Moscow.** *Local people go to GUM for shopping. The buildings are fine – but there are still queues and shortages in Russian shops. GUM is short for Government Department Store in Russian.*

Trans-Siberian Railway

It takes a week to cross Russia by train, and you must change your watch seven times. Here is the distance chart and timetable (only the main stops are shown).

Distance in km	Town	Time (at Moscow)	Day
0	Moscow	15.05	1
957	Kirov	04.00	2
1818	Yekaterinburg	16.25	2
2716	Omsk	03.13	3
3343	Novosibirsk	10.44	3
4104	Krasnoyarsk	22.31	3
5184	Irkutsk	16.23	4
5647	Ulan Ude	00.02	5
6204	Chita	09.23	5
7313	Skovorodino	05.20	6
8531	Khabarovsk	01.10	7
9297	Vladivostok	13.30★	7

★This is 20.30 local time at Vladivostok.

Don't forget to allow another week if you want to come back!

А	Б	В	Г	Д	Е	Ё	Ж	З	И	Й	К	Л	М	Н	О	П	Р	С	Т	У	Ф	Х	Ц	Ч	Ш	Щ	Ъ	Э	Ю	Я
A	B	V	G	D	E	YO	ZH	Z	I	Y	K	L	M	N	O	P	R	S	T	U	F	KH	TS	CH	SH	SHCH	–	E	YU	YA

MIDDLE EAST

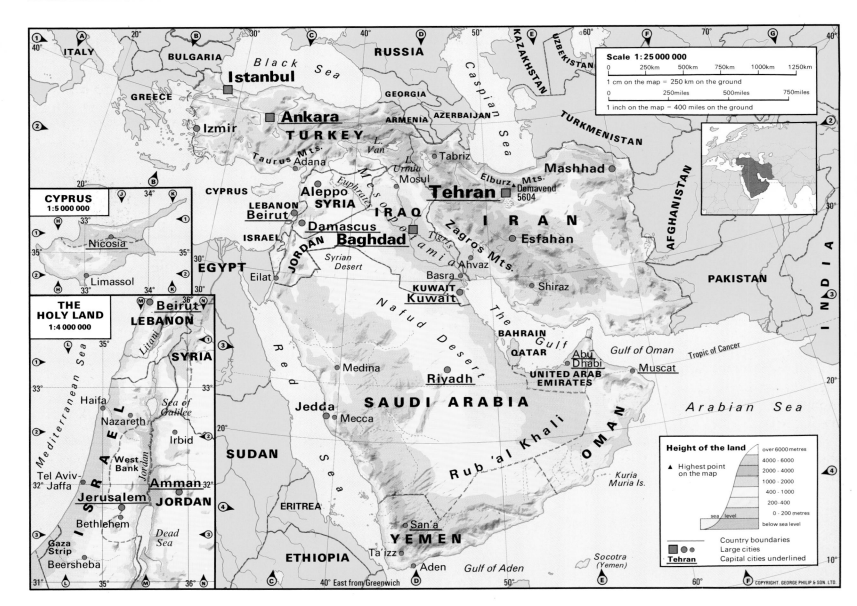

CYPRUS
1:5 000 000

THE HOLY LAND
1:4 000 000

Scale 1:25 000 000

| 0 | 250km | 500km | 750km | 1000km | 1250km |

1 cm on the map = 250 km on the ground

| 0 | 250miles | 500miles | 750miles |

1 inch on the map = 400 miles on the ground

Height of the land

	over 6000 metres
	4000 - 6000
▲ Highest point on the map	2000 - 4000
	1000 - 2000
	400 - 1000
	200 - 400
	0 - 200 metres
sea level	below sea level

	Country boundaries
■ ●●	Large cities
Tehran	Capital cities underlined

COPYRIGHT. GEORGE PHILIP & SON. LTD.

Holy cities of the Middle East.

◀ **Jerusalem:** Jews worship at the Wailing Wall, all that remains of the Jewish temple. Jerusalem is a holy city for people of three religions: Judaism, Christianity and Islam. People of all three religions live here and pilgrims and tourists visit the city.

▶ **Mecca** is the holiest city of Islam: it is where the prophet Mohammed was born. Muslims come from many countries to worship here.

Lands of the books

Three great religions started in the Middle East: Judaism, Christianity and Islam.

The Jewish scriptures are written in Hebrew. This is the world's oldest written language still in use today and reads from right to left across the page.

The Christian Bible consists of the Jewish scriptures (the Old Testament), plus the New Testament, which was originally written in Greek.

The Koran is the holy book of Islam. It is written in Arabic, which is also read from right to left.

▼ **The Jewish scriptures are written in Hebrew.**

אֵשִׁית בָּרָא אֱלֹהִים אֵת הַשָּׁמַיִם וְאֵת
ה תֹהוּ וָבֹהוּ וְחֹשֶׁךְ עַל־פְּנֵי תְהֹם
פֶת עַל־פְּנֵי הַמָּיִם: וַיֹּאמֶר אֱלֹהִים
: וַיַּרְא אֱלֹהִים אֶת־הָאוֹר כִּי־טוֹב וַיַּב
־ וּבֵין הַחֹשֶׁךְ: וַיִּקְרָא אֱלֹהִים ׀ לָא
: לַיְלָה וַיְהִי־עֶרֶב וַיְהִי־בֹקֶר יוֹם אֶחָד

▼ **The Koran is written in Arabic.**

مِن دُونِ اللَّهِ وَزَيَّنَ لَهُمُ الشَّيْطَانُ أَعْمَالَهُمْ
فَصَدَّهُمْ عَنِ السَّبِيلِ فَهُمْ لَا يَهْتَدُونَ
أَلَّا يَسْجُدُوا لِلَّهِ الَّذِي يُخْرِجُ الْخَبْءَ فِي
السَّمَاوَاتِ وَالْأَرْضِ وَيَعْلَمُ مَا تُخْفُونَ وَ

▲ *Camels, desert – and oil.*
The photograph above, taken in Iran, shows camels in the desert . . . a view that has not changed for centuries. But the flares and smoke in the distance are a clue to the biggest change in the Middle East: oil. Oil is pumped out from deep underground, and piped to ports for export to many countries in Europe, Asia and Africa. It is used for diesel, petroleum, paraffin and chemicals.

The 'Middle East' is another name for 'south-west Asia'. It is the part of Asia which is closest to Europe and Africa. In fact, Turkey is partly in Europe. Of all the countries on this map, Turkey has the most people.

Most of the Middle East is semi-desert or desert. Yet many great civilizations have existed here, such as the Assyrian, the Babylonian and the Persian. Their monuments are found in the fertile valleys of the largest rivers, the Tigris and the Euphrates.

Scarce water is used to irrigate crops in some places. In others, herds of sheep and goats are kept. Dates from Iraq come from desert oases; oranges come from irrigated land in Israel.

▲ *Progress in Qatar.* The big bulldozer was imported from England, to help build the new road. In the background you can see new skyscrapers and a big crane. Oil has made some countries in the Middle East very rich, especially Saudi Arabia, Kuwait and Qatar.

◄ *Winnowing wheat in Turkey.*
The gentle evening breeze separates the grain from the chaff: the heavier grain falls down, while the lighter chaff blows away. Winnowing is hard work! It has been done by hand for thousands of years: the old methods are still commonly used in many parts of the Middle East.

SOUTH ASIA

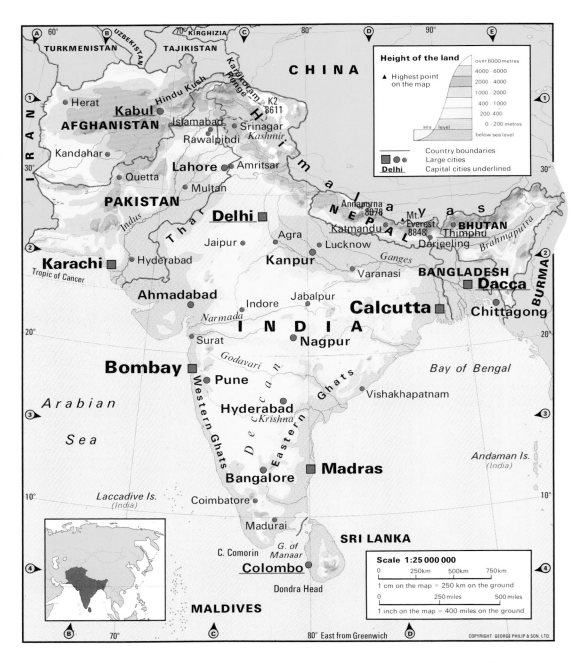

The world's highest mountains appear on this map, including Mount Everest. The Himalayas form a great mountain chain which joins on to other high mountain areas, such as the Hindu Kush.

More than 1000 million people live in south Asia. The deserts and mountains do not have many people, but the river valleys, plains and plateaus are crowded.

Afghanistan, Bhutan and **Nepal** are rugged, mountainous countries.

Bangladesh is very different: it is mostly flat, low-lying land where the great rivers Ganges and Brahmaputra reach the sea.

Pakistan is a desert country, but the River Indus is used to irrigate crops.

India is the largest country. It stretches 3300 kilometres from the Himalayas to Cape Comorin. Until 1947, Pakistan and Bangladesh were part of the Indian Empire, ruled by Britain.

Sri Lanka is an island country off the south coast of India.

The Maldives are a chain of islands in the Indian Ocean.

Sri Lanka means Resplendent Isle. This country used to be called Ceylon.

▶ *Tea* is an important crop in the hills where there is plenty of rain. Women pick the young leaves from the bushes (right), then they are dried and crushed and packed into tea-chests. Ceylon tea (left) is one of Sri Lanka's most important exports. Where does the tea you drink come from?

▲ **Planting rice, Bangladesh.**
These men are planting out rice seedlings in the wet soil. Sometimes monsoon floods can wash away the seedlings.

Rice is an important food crop in south Asia. It grows best where the land is flat, and where the weather is hot and wet. The seeds are planted in a 'nursery' bed just before the monsoon rains are due. When the fields are flooded, the seedlings are planted in the mud. In a good year, rice grows in the wet fields and is ready for harvesting after four or five months. If the monsoon fails and there is a drought, the seedlings will shrivel up. If the rice crop fails, many people go hungry. Where irrigation is available, the farmer can control the water supply and may be able to grow two rice crops a year.

Religion is very important in the lives of people in south Asia. Hinduism is the oldest religion, and most people in India and Nepal are Hindus. Buddhism began in India, but only Sri Lanka and Bhutan are mainly Buddhist today. Afghanistan, Pakistan and Bangladesh are Islamic countries. Many Sikhs live in northern India; there are also Christian groups in all these countries.

▲ **India's flag** *shows that people of different religions are united in one country. The orange stripe is for Hindus; the green for Muslims; and the white for peace, with the wheel of Ashoka for Buddhists.*

▼ **Wool for carpets.** *This lady in northern India is winding wool which will be used to make carpets. She sits in the courtyard of her house, where the ploughs and pots and pans are also kept.*

The monsoon

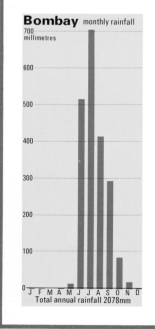

Total annual rainfall 2078mm

Most rain falls in one season, called the monsoon. In Bombay the monsoon begins in June (left) and the rain pours down for a few weeks (right). There are heavy showers in August and September, and then hardly any more rain until next June. From October to March the weather is cool and dry, then it gets hotter and hotter until the monsoon rains begin.

North-east India and Bangladesh have even more rain than Bombay. But large areas of north-west India are desert.

SOUTH-EAST ASIA

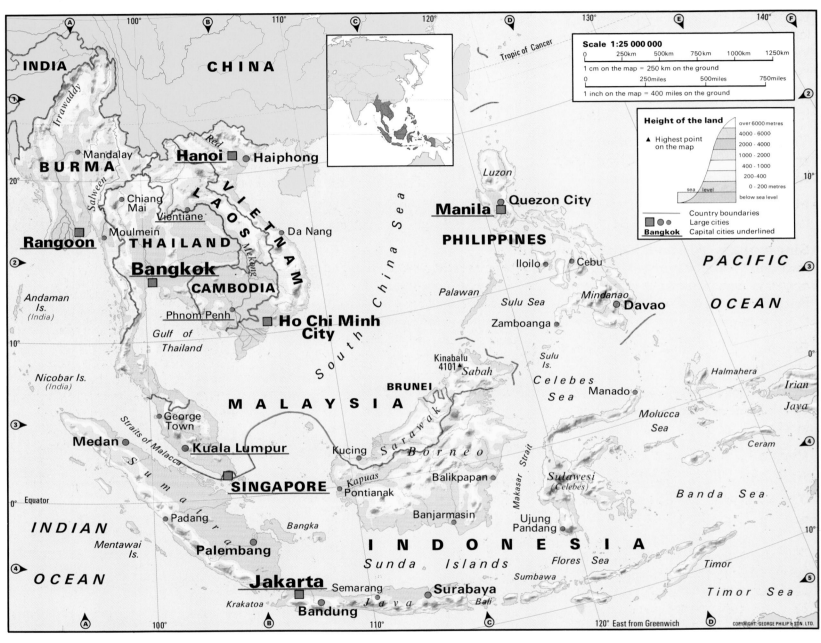

INDIA

CHINA

Tropic of Cancer

Scale 1:25 000 000

1 cm on the map = 250 km on the ground

1 inch on the map = 400 miles on the ground

Height of the land
- ▲ Highest point on the map
- over 6000 metres
- 4000 - 6000
- 2000 - 4000
- 1000 - 2000
- 400 - 1000
- 200 - 400
- 0 - 200 metres
- below sea level

Country boundaries
■ ●● Large cities
■ **Bangkok** Capital cities underlined

Irrawaddy

• Mandalay

Hanoi ■ • Haiphong

BURMA

Red

Luzon

Salween

• Chiang Mai

Manila ■ • **Quezon City**

Vientiane

LAOS

VIETNAM

Rangoon ■ Moulmein • Da Nang

THAILAND

PHILIPPINES

Bangkok ■

CAMBODIA

South China Sea

Iloilo • • Cebu

PACIFIC

Andaman Is. (India)

Phnom Penh

Ho Chi Minh City ■

Palawan

Sulu Sea

Mindanao • **Davao**

OCEAN

Gulf of Thailand

Zamboanga

Nicobar Is. (India)

Kinabalu 4101 ▲ *Sabah*

Sulu Is.

Celebes Sea

• Manado

BRUNEI

Halmahera

Irian Jaya

M A L A Y S I A

Sarawak

B o r n e o

Molucca Sea

Ceram

• George Town

Kucing

Medan •

Straits of Malacca

Makasar Strait

Sulawesi (Celebes)

Kuala Lumpur

Balikpapan •

Banda Sea

S u m a t r a

Kapuas

SINGAPORE ■ • Pontianak

0° Equator

• Padang

Banjarmasin •

Ujung Pandang •

INDIAN

Mentawai Is.

Bangka

I N D O N E S I A

Flores Sea

Timor

OCEAN

Palembang •

Sunda Islands

Sumbawa

Timor Sea

Jakarta ■ Semarang

Surabaya •

Krakatoa *J a v a* *Bali*

Bandung

120° East from Greenwich

COPYRIGHT GEORGE PHILIP & SON. LTD.

Stamps from South-east Asia.
Singapore *has four main religions:*

| Christian church ▼ | Buddhist temple ▼ | Islamic mosque ▼ | Hindu temple ▼ |

▶ ***Laos.*** *Elephants carry huge logs from the jungle. Laos was once called Lanxang – 'land of a million elephants'.*

◀ ***Vietnam.*** *Children learn to draw a map of their country. North and South Vietnam were united in 1976 after many years of fighting.*

The Equator crosses South-east Asia, so it is always hot. Heavy tropical rainstorms are common, too.

The mainland and most of the islands are very mountainous. The mountains are covered with thick tropical forest (look at the stamp of Laos). These areas are very difficult to reach and have few people. The large rivers are important routes inland. Their valleys and deltas are very crowded indeed.

Indonesia is the biggest country. It used to be the Dutch East Indies.

The Philippines is another large group of islands, south of China. They were Spanish until 1898.

Malaysia includes part of the mainland and most of northern Borneo.

Singapore is an island at the tip of mainland Malaysia, but a separate country. Both countries were once British and are members of the Commonwealth.

Brunei is a very small but a very rich country.

Burma (Myanmar) was part of the Indian Empire. It became independent in 1948.

Vietnam, **Laos** and **Cambodia** were once called French Indo-China.

Thailand has always been independent, and has a king.

▼ *Floating market in Thailand.* Farmers bring their fruit and vegetables to a Bangkok market by boat. On some boats there are fish which are cooked on the boat and sold for lunch.

▲ *Harvesting rice. Rice grows on terraces cut into the mountainside in Bali. Each terrace is sown and harvested by hand. Bali is a small island east of Java. Some people claim that it is the most beautiful island of Indonesia, and all the world!*

▼ *A Thai schoolbook. This page from a children's book about Thailand shows a man harvesting pineapples. Can you see how he waters the fields from the river?*

Fact box: Indonesia

Did you know that Indonesia has the **fourth largest population** in the world (see page 9); is the **world's greatest archipelago** – a group of 13,000 islands, which stretches for 5600 kilometres; has **more active volcanoes** than any other country (77); suffered the **world's biggest recorded bang** – when the island of Krakatoa blew up in a volcanic eruption in 1883.

ประเทศ ไทย ของ ฉัน มี ต้น ข้าว มี ต้น ผัก
และ มี ต้น ผลไม้ มาก มาย

**In Thailand we have plenty of
rice, vegetables and fruit.**

CHINA
AND NEIGHBOURS

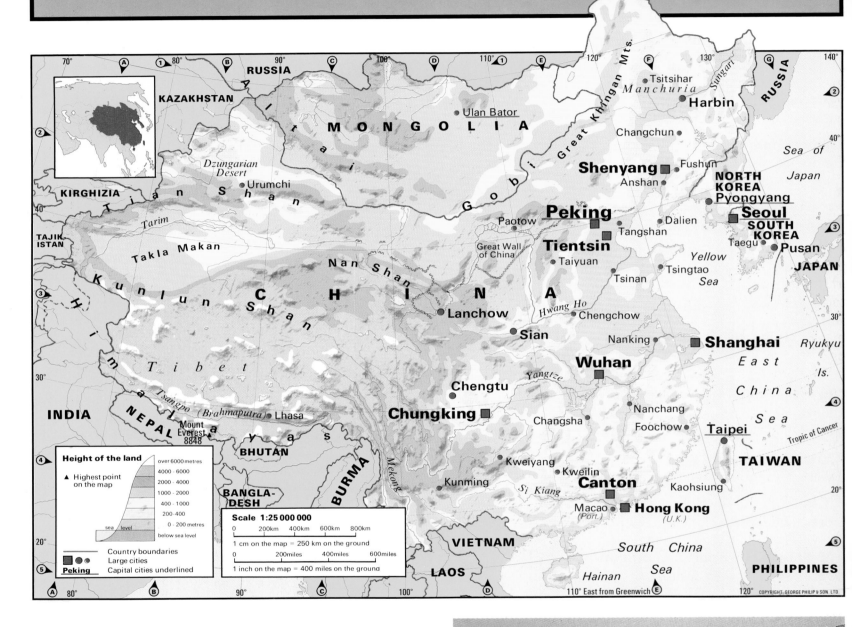

Height of the land

▲ Highest point on the map

over 6000 metres
4000 - 6000
2000 - 4000
1000 - 2000
400 - 1000
200 - 400
0 - 200 metres
below sea level

Country boundaries
Large cities
Peking Capital cities underlined

Scale 1:25 000 000

0   200km 400km 600km 800km

1 cm on the map = 250 km on the ground

0   200miles   400miles   600miles

1 inch on the map = 400 miles on the ground

▶ *China's amazing mountains. Both the stamp and the photograph show the amazing shapes of the limestone mountains in southern China. The mountains that look 'unreal' in Chinese paintings really are real! It is almost impossible to travel through this area except by boat. The heavy rain has slowly dissolved the limestone to make these picturesque mountains.*

The river is the Kwei, which flows through Kweilin, an old city dating back to the sixth century.

China has over a billion people (1,134,000,000) – more than any other country in the world. The map shows that there are many high mountains in China, such as the huge plateau of Tibet and the rugged mountains of the south-west where the Giant Pandas live. Not many people live in these mountains, nor in the deserts of the north, near Mongolia. So the lower land of eastern China is *very* crowded indeed. Rice grows well south of the River Yangtze. North of the Yangtze, where the winters are colder, wheat and maize are important food crops, but it is hard to grow enough.

▼ *Building a reservoir.*
Everybody, male and female, pulls a heavy cart of rocks to make a new dam across a river. The dam will provide water for power and for irrigation – and it will control flooding too. China has made great progress with projects like this, which use lots of people and few machines. Long ago the Great Wall of China was built in this way to keep out China's enemies.

China's neighbours

Mongolia is a huge desert country, three times bigger than Spain. It is the world's emptiest country: there are fewer than 3 million people.

North Korea is a Communist country. It separated from South Korea in the Korean War in 1953.

South Korea has over 43 million people – more than Canada and Australia put together!

Taiwan is an island country which used to be called Formosa, or Nationalist China. It is not Communist and is not part of the rest of China.

▼ Hong Kong. Most of Hong Kong was part of China until 1898 and is Chinese again from 1997 onwards. For 99 years the British ruled Hong Kong.

The photograph shows big new skyscrapers standing on the hills. Six million people live in this small, crowded territory. The hydrofoil is going to **Macao,** a nearby Portugese colony.

◄ *Traffic in Tientsin.* *Rush hour in Chinese cities is not the same as in New York or London: there are hardly any cars. People travel on foot, or by bicycle or bus. Tientsin is a big port in northern China and is one of the largest cities in the country.*

Fact box

* One person out of every five people in the world is Chinese.

* This century's worst earthquake happened in Tangshan in 1976. This is in the crowded part of China, so many people were killed.

* The Chinese invented an earthquake detector 1800 years ago. They also invented the compass, paper and printing.

*The Chinese have been eating with chopsticks for over 3000 years!

* The place furthest from the open sea is in China: the Dzungarian Desert, 2400 kilometres from the sea. A man from Norwich in England who cycled there said it is 'hot and horrible'!

* The highest plateau in the world is Tibet. Its average height is nearly 5000 metres above sea-level – as high as Mont Blanc (see page 27)! Lhasa, Tibet, has the world's highest airport, at 4363 metres. The runway is extra long as there is so little air pressure to help aircraft take off. (See map: C4.)

* The Chinese language has many dialects: the commonest is Mandarin. Each sound has four tones; words are written using thousands of different characters. Chinese used to be written from top to bottom of the page; now it is written from left to right.

*The Great Wall of China can be seen from the Moon! It was over 5000 kilometres long, but some parts no longer exist. Building started 2000 years ago. (See map: D3.)

JAPAN

▲ **Bullet train.** *Japan's 'bullet trains' go like a bullet from a gun! The trains run on new tracks with no sharp curves to slow them down. They provide a superb service except when there is an earthquake warning. When that happens, the trains have to go more slowly, to be safe.*

Japan is quite a small country: it is smaller than France or Spain. Canada is 27 times as big as Japan! But Japan has a big population – about 124,000,000. This is over twice as many people as France, and five times as many as Canada.

People talk of the 'Japanese miracle'. This small country is mostly mountains, has very few mines and hardly any oil, yet it has become the world's biggest producer of televisions, radios, music centres, cameras, trucks, ships and many other things. Japanese cars and computers are admired throughout the world. There are booming cities in the south of Japan, with highly skilled, hard-working people. Many of them live in the city suburbs and travel to work in overcrowded trains. Most Japanese families have small, space-saving homes. The main room is usually a living room by day, then the beds are unrolled for the night and packed away next morning. But away from the cities, most of Japan is still beautiful and peaceful.

Many mountains are volcanoes. There are 54 active volcanoes, and over 100 others. The northernmost island, Hokkaido, is much less crowded. It has very cold winters, and even the summers are too cold for growing rice. But in the south of Japan, rice is the main food crop. Some of the hillsides look like giant steps, because they are terraced to make flat fields.

▲ **Huge baskets for live fish.** *Fish are caught and then stored in these huge baskets. The Japanese eat more fish than people in any other country, but sadly the seas near Japan have been polluted by industry. Big Japanese trawlers fish thousands of kilometres away from home.*

▼ **Mount Fuji in winter.** *Fujiyama (Mount Fuji) is Japan's most famous mountain. It is an old volcano, 3776 metres high. In winter, the upper slopes are covered with snow. The 'bullet trains' pass Mount Fuji on their high-speed journey from Tokyo to Nagoya and Osaka.*

Horyu Temple, at Nara

The beautiful temple on the right is called a pagoda. Japanese pagodas are carefully preserved. Their unusual shape originally came partly from Indian temples and partly from Chinese temples. This is one of many Japanese stamps on the theme of national treasures. Nippon is Japanese for Japan.

Scale 1: 7 500 000

0	75km	150km	225km	300km	375km	450km

1 cm on the map = 75 km on the ground

0	75miles	150miles	225miles	300miles

1 inch on the map = 120 miles on the ground

Height of the land

▲ Highest point on the map

- over 6000 metres
- 4000 - 6000
- 2000 - 4000
- 1000 - 2000
- 400 - 1000
- 200-400
- 0 - 200 metres
- below sea level!

sea level

Country boundaries
Large cities
Tokyo Capital city underlined

AFRICA

◄ **Children in Ghana.** *Everywhere in Africa, there are lots of children. The fathers of these children are fishermen: in the background you can see big dug-out canoes. The canoes are made from the huge trees of the rainforest, and can cope with big waves in the Gulf of Guinea. These children get plenty of fish to eat, but in some parts of Africa hunger is a major problem.*

Most of the countries of Africa have quite small populations – except for Nigeria and Egypt. But everywhere the population is growing fast. It is difficult to provide enough schools and clinics for all the children and there are not enough good jobs. So African countries are trying hard to improve fishing, mining and industry.

Fact box: Africa

Area 30,319,000 square kilometres
Highest point Mount Kilimanjaro (Tanzania), 5895 metres
Lowest point Shores of Lake Assal (Djibouti), 155 metres below sea-level
Longest river Nile, 6670 kilometres (also a *world* record)
Largest lake Lake Victoria (East Africa), 69,484 square kilometres
Biggest country Sudan, 2,505,813 square kilometres
Smallest countries
  Mainland: Gambia, 11,295 square kilometres;
  Islands: Seychelles, 308 square kilometres
  (see page 9)

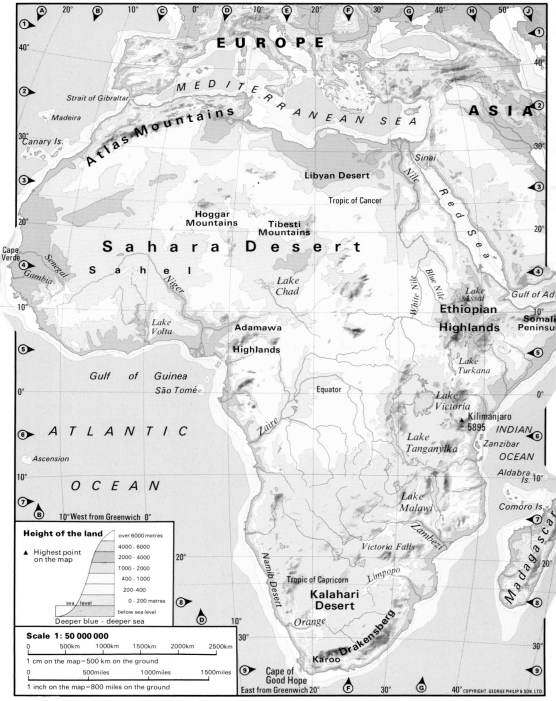

◄ **The pyramids of Egypt.** The pyramids are tombs which were built by slaves over 4000 years ago. They are still the biggest buildings in the whole of Africa. They are near the River Nile, in the Sahara Desert. These camels are for the tourists that visit the pyramids.

Imagine travelling southwards across Africa, along the 20°E line of longitude. You start in Libya. Your first 1000 kilometres will be across the great Sahara Desert (where you *must* travel in winter) – sand, rock and the high rugged Tibesti Mountains. Then you reach thorn bushes, in the semi-desert Sahel area of Chad.

By 15°N you are into savanna – very long grass and scattered trees. You cross the country known as CAR for short. The land becomes greener and at about 5°N you reach the equatorial rainforest ... a real jungle! You are now in Zaïre.

Then the same story happens in reverse – savanna in Angola; then semi-desert (the Kalahari and the Karoo). Finally you reach the mountains and coast of South Africa – a journey of nearly 8000 kilometres.

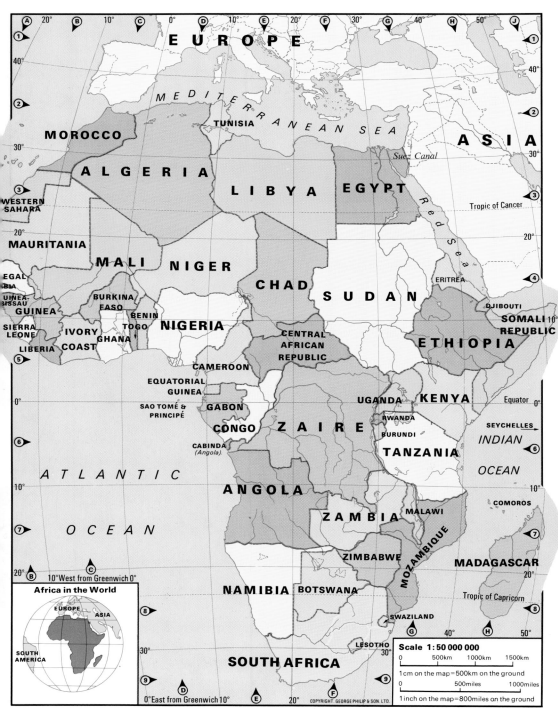

Where do the country names come from?

Chad From Lake Chad

Gambia, Niger, Nigeria From big rivers in these countries

Ghana, Benin, Mali Names of great empires in West Africa a long time ago

Ivory Coast Ivory, from the tusks of elephants, used to be traded along this coast

Namibia From the *Namib* Desert

Sierra Leone 'Lion Mountain' in Portuguese (named by explorers)

Tanzania From *Tan*ganyika (the mainland) and the island of *Zan*zibar

NORTH AFRICA

Most of North Africa is desert – but not all. The coastlines and mountains of north-west Africa get winter rain: good crops are grown, and the area is popular all year with tourists from Europe. These countries are Islamic. **Morocco** has the oldest university in the world: the Islamic University in Fez.

Oil has made **Libya** rich. The other countries still have much poverty. The Sahel states, at the southern edge of the Sahara, are among the poorest countries in the world. They had severe famines in the 1970s and 1980s.

Egypt has the biggest population of any North African country. Its capital, Cairo, is one of the biggest cities in the world. The River Nile brings water to the valley and delta. The land is carefully farmed (with irrigation) and crowded with people; the rest of Egypt is almost empty. The map shows that part of the desert is *below* sea-level.

The lack of rain has helped to preserve many of the marvellous monuments, palaces and tombs built by the ancient Egyptians. The pyramids at Giza, near Cairo, are 4500 years old (see page 53). They are the only one of the Seven Wonders of the ancient world still surviving.

◄ *Oasis, Algeria. The water allows date-palms to grow well. But in the background, great sand-dunes loom on the skyline: if they advance, they may cover the oasis one day. In the foreground there is rock desert which is more common than sand desert.*

▼ **Huge sand-dunes, Libya.** *Land-Rover tracks can be seen in the foreground. But no vehicles can cross the huge, steep sand-dunes in the background. The Land-Rover has stopped in front of the dunes. Only about a tenth of the Sahara Desert is made up of sand-dunes. Other parts are gravel desert, rock desert, salt desert, dried-up lakes, and desert mountains.*

▲ **Camels at market, Tunisia.** *Camels are ideal for deserts: they can survive for a long time without water, by relying on the fat in their humps. They can carry heavy loads, and can walk well on soft sand. But nowadays, lorries are taking over from camels for long-distance travel.*

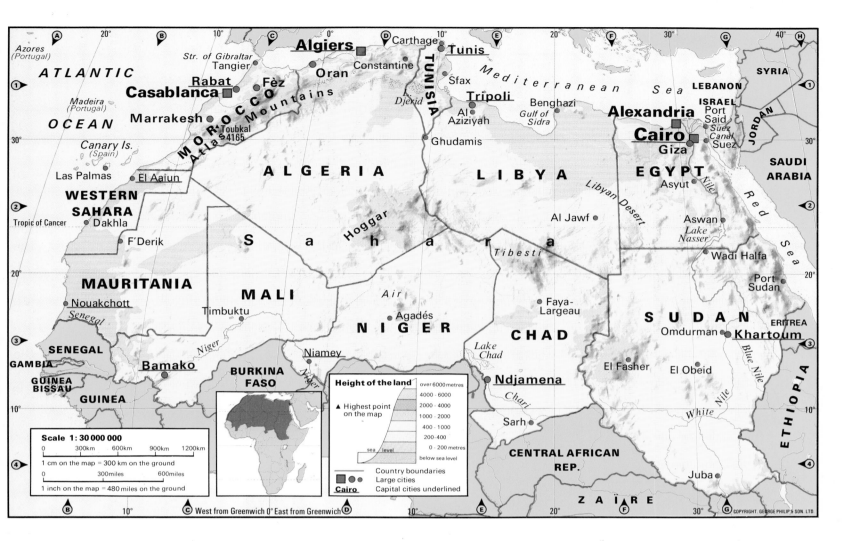

Scale 1: 30 000 000

0	300km	600km	900km	1200km

1 cm on the map = 300 km on the ground

0	300miles	600miles

1 inch on the map = 480 miles on the ground

Height of the land

	over 6000 metres
	4000 - 6000
▲ Highest point on the map	2000 - 4000
	1000 - 2000
	400 - 1000
	200 - 400
sea level	0 - 200 metres
	below sea level

Country boundaries
Large cities
Cairo Capital cities underlined

West from Greenwich 0° East from Greenwich

COPYRIGHT. GEORGE PHILIP'S SON. LTD.

Puzzle picture

This is a satellite photograph of part of the Sahara Desert in southern Libya. Who has drawn these circles in the desert, and why? How have they become green? Why are some circles more green than others?

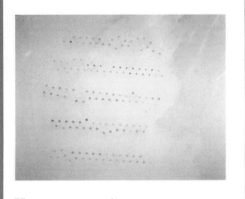

Have a guess – then turn to page 96.

▼ **The Suez Canal** (see map: G1). This container ship is travelling through the desert of Egypt! The Suez Canal was dug in 1859–69 by Arabs, organized by a Frenchman, Ferdinand de Lesseps. Before the canal was dug, the route by sea from Europe to India and the Far East was around the whole of Africa.

For almost a century, the canal was a very important route; but now aeroplanes have taken over almost all the passenger traffic, and many oil-tankers are much too big to go through it. Today it is mostly used for freight travelling from Asia to Europe.

Saharan records

The Sahara is the **biggest desert** in the world. It is over 8 million square kilometres in size. From west to east it is over 5000 kilometres; from north to south it extends about 2000 kilometres and it is still growing.

The **hottest shade temperature** ever recorded, 58°C, was in Al Aziziyah, Libya, in 1922.

The **sunniest** place in the world, over 4300 hours of sunshine per year, is in the eastern Sahara.

The **highest sand-dunes** in the world, 430 metres high, are in east central Algeria.

The **longest river** in the world is the River Nile, 6670 kilometres. (How strange that a desert should have the world's longest river!)

55

WEST AFRICA

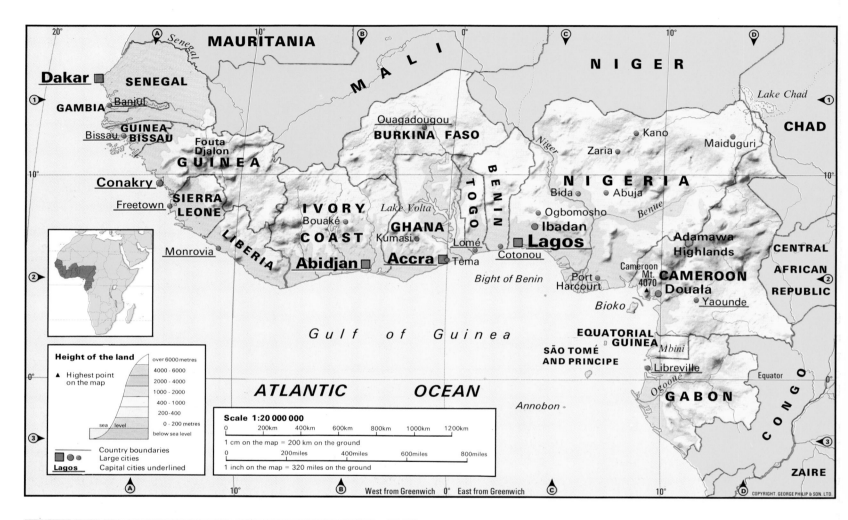

Height of the land

- ▲ Highest point on the map

over 6000 metres
4000 - 6000
2000 - 4000
1000 - 2000
400 - 1000
200-400
0 - 200 metres
below sea level

sea level

Country boundaries
Large cities
Lagos Capital cities underlined

Scale 1:20 000 000

| 0 | 200km | 400km | 600km | 800km | 1000km | 1200km |

1 cm on the map = 200 km on the ground

| 0 | 200miles | 400miles | 600miles | 800miles |

1 inch on the map = 320 miles on the ground

West from Greenwich 0° East from Greenwich

There are lots of countries in West Africa. In the last 300 years, European countries grabbed parts of the coastline and later they took over the inland areas as well. Now, all the countries are independent, but still use the language of those who once ruled them. English, French, Spanish or Portuguese is spoken. Many Africans speak a European language as well as one or more African languages.

Nigeria is the largest and most important country in West Africa. It has over 119 million people – more than any other African country. Although English is the official language, there are about 240 others in Nigeria!

◀ **Market day.** Red peppers for sale in Bida, Nigeria. Red peppers are very popular in West Africa – they give a strong flavour in cooking. Markets are important in both towns and villages in all the countries of West Africa. Most of the selling is done by women.

Puzzle picture

Why is this man building all these mounds? Make a guess – then turn to page 96.

◀ *Extinct volcanoes. Long ago these mountains in Cameroon were volcanoes. Now only the cores of the volcanoes are left: the rest has been eroded away. Notice the thatched roofs of the houses.*

Everywhere in West Africa there is rapid progress. Most children now go to primary school, and the capital cities have televisions and airports. But many people are still very poor.

The southern part of West Africa, near the Equator, is forested. The tall trees are being felled for their hardwood. Many crops are grown in the forest area and sold overseas: cocoa (for chocolate-making); coffee, pineapples and bananas; rubber (for car and lorry tyres). The main food crops are root crops, such as cassava and yams.

Further north, the trees thin out and there is savanna. The tall grass with some trees is suitable for cattle farming. There are big herds of cattle, and beautiful leather goods are on sale in the markets. Cotton and groundnuts (peanuts) are grown in the savanna lands. The main food crops are grass-like: rice, maize, sorghum and millet.

▶ *Yeji ferry, Ghana. This big ferry carries lorries, cars, people and their heavy loads across Lake Volta. This man-made lake flooded Ghana's main road to the north. You can see trees that died as the water rose in the new lake.*

▶ *Harvesting rice in Ghana. This view could be in Europe or North America! Huge combine harvesters are reaping rice on a large farm in northern Ghana. But most farms are very small.*

EAST AND CENTRAL AFRICA

▲ **Fishermen, Zaïre.** *Each one of these fishing boats is made from a single tree, hollowed out with an axe. They are called dug-out canoes – there is no danger of a leak in the boat!*

▲ **Picking tea: Nandi, Kenya.** *The tender young leaves are picked by hand and taken to a factory where they will be dried and crushed. Tea grows well in the highlands of East Africa. It is an important export of Kenya.*

Bus services in Africa

Bus journeys in Africa are exciting, and the fares are very cheap, but many roads are very bumpy! 'Safari' is the Swahili word for 'journey'. This bus ticket is for a journey (safari) in Tanzania from Moshi to Dar es Salaam.

Masama Cliff Bus Service
S. L. P. 1989, MOSHI, Tanzania
Safari za Moshi ——— Dar es Salaam
Tarehe ya Safari Na Kiti
22/12/87
No. 1858
Shs 43.81

Central Africa is mostly lowland, with magnificent trees in the tropical rainforest in Zaïre and Congo. Some timber is used for buildings and canoes (see photograph above left); some is exported. The cleared land can grow many tropical crops.

East Africa is mostly high savanna land with long grass, and scattered trees. Some parts are reserved for wild animals; in other parts, there are large farms for export crops such as coffee and tea. But in most of East Africa, the people keep cattle and grow crops for their own needs.

The Somali Republic, Djibouti and the lowland parts of Ethiopia are desert areas, but the mountains of Ethiopia get plenty of rain. There have been terrible wars and famines in Ethiopia and Somalia. In 1992–3, the UN and USA helped with peace-keeping and food deliveries in Somalia.

In all these countries the population is growing fast. There is much poverty and people are moving to the cities. But there are also many signs of development: new farm projects, new ports and roads, and new schools, except where wars prevent development.

▼ **The Masai people** *live mainly by herding cattle on the plains near the border of Kenya and Tanzania. These teenage boys are dressed as warriors. They learn to hunt and to guard the cattle.*

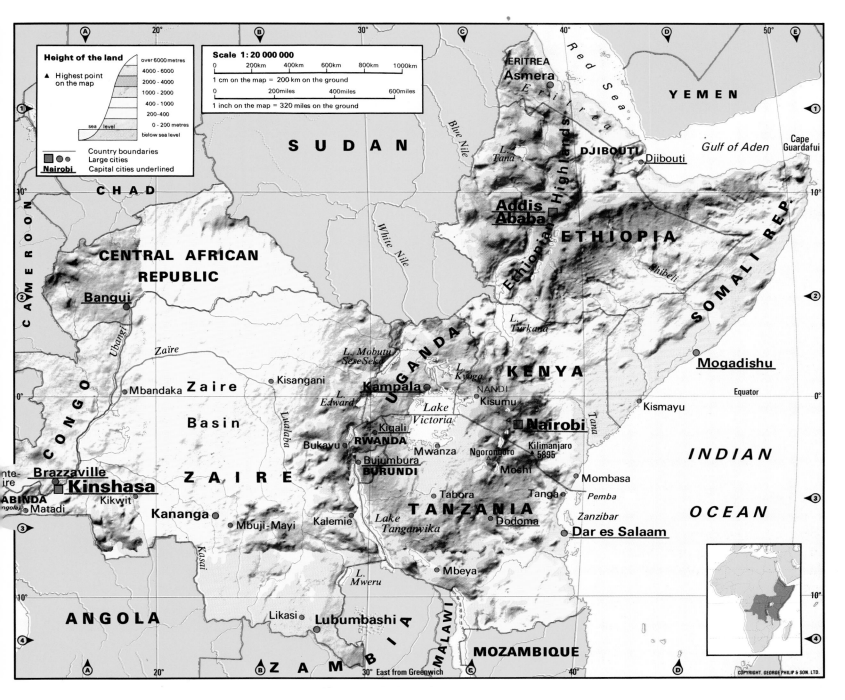

▶ **Zebra and wildebeest** at Ngorongoro, Tanzania. People come from all over the world to go on wildlife safaris in East Africa. This lake is in the crater of an old volcano. Animals gather to drink the water, because there is no other water nearby in the long dry season.

The game reserves of East Africa are carefully managed to conserve the wildlife. Elephants, lions and giraffes are only 'shot' by cameras now: guns are banned The money spent by tourists is very important for Kenya and Tanzania.

SOUTHERN AFRICA

Most of southern Africa is a high, flat plateau. The rivers cannot be used by ships because of big waterfalls like the Victoria Falls (see page 61). But the rivers can be useful. Two huge dams have been built on the River Zambezi – at Kariba (in Zambia) and at Cabora Bassa (in Mozambique). The map shows the lakes behind each dam. The power of the falling water is used to make electricity.

Angola and **Mozambique** used to be Portuguese colonies, and Portuguese is still their official language – though many different African languages are spoken, too. Most of the other countries shown on the map have English as their official language.

Notice that many southern African countries are land-locked: they have no coastline. The railways leading to the ports in neighbouring countries are very important. Copper from Zambia and Botswana is sent abroad in this way.

The **Republic of South Africa** is the wealthiest country in Africa. It has the richest gold mine in the world, and also priceless diamond mines. But most of the black people are very poor. For many years, they were kept apart from the rich white people who used to rule the country.

Namibia and **Botswana** are dry areas, with small numbers of people. Some of the rivers in this area never reach the sea. The map on page 61 shows big swamps and 'salt pans': these are the places where the river water evaporates.

Madagascar is one of the world's biggest islands. It has wonderful forests and wildlife – but several species are under threat.

A village in Zambia

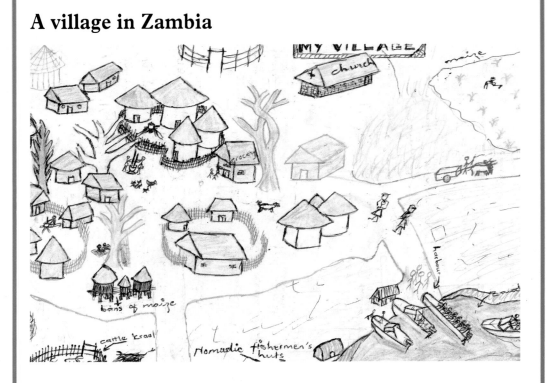

Sianga drew this picture of her village during a lesson at her school in Zambia. Her village is close to the River Zambezi in the west of the country.

▼ *An unfriendly notice* *in three languages on a white-owned poultry farm in South Africa.*

▲ *A baobab tree.* *In almost all southern Africa there is a long, hot dry season. The baobab tree is good at surviving a long drought. It has a specially fat trunk and main branches which hold water like a sponge and help to keep it alive.*

World records

▶ The **Victoria Falls** are on the River Zambezi, at the border of Zambia and Zimbabwe. Africans call the falls *Mosi-oi-tunya* – 'the smoke that thunders'. They were named after the English Queen Victoria by the explorer David Livingstone.

The world's **oldest mines** are in Swaziland. Iron ore was mined here 43,000 years ago.

The world's **deepest mine** is the gold mine at Carletonville, South Africa. It is 3777 metres deep.

▶ The huge diamond mine shown here is in Namibia. The desert is scraped away to reach the rock beneath, where diamonds are found. The yellow lorry is huge, but it looks very small in this vast mine.

Diamonds are mined in several countries in southern Africa. The world's biggest diamond was found near Pretoria, South Africa, in 1905.

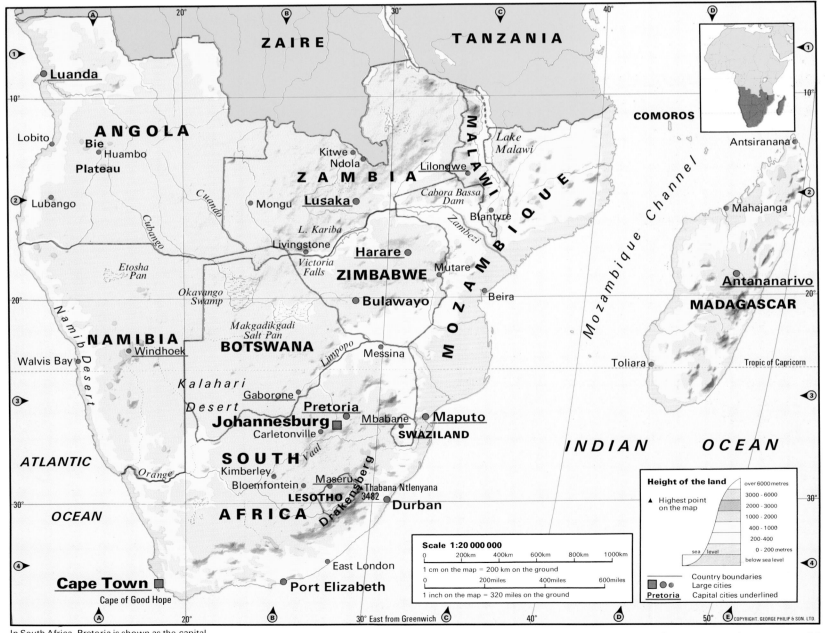

In South Africa, Pretoria is shown as the capital but the parliament meets in Cape Town.

NORTH AMERICA

North America includes many Arctic islands, a huge mainland area (quite narrow in Central America) and the islands in the Caribbean Sea. The map shows the great mountain ranges which are the most impressive feature of this continent. Almost all the west is mountainous. These are mostly fold mountains but the highest peaks are volcanoes. The Appalachian Mountains in the east are also fold mountains. And the island chains of the north-west (the Aleutian Islands) and the south-east (the West Indies) are the tops of underwater ranges.

▼ **Fruit market, Barbados, West Indies.** *The West Indies have hot sunshine and plenty of rain. This is an ideal climate for growing excellent fruit. Which types of fruit can you recognize in this market? (Answer on page 96.)*

Height of the land

over 6000 metres
4000 - 6000
2000 - 4000
1000 - 2000
400 - 1000
200 - 400
0 - 200 metres

sea / level · below sea level

Deeper blue - deeper sea
▲ Highest point on the map

Scale 1 : 50 000 000

| 0 | 500km | 1000km | 1500km | 2000km | 2500km |

1 cm on the map = 500 km on the ground

| 0 | 500miles | 1000miles | 1500miles |

1 inch on the map = 800 miles on the ground

The political map of North America is quite a simple one. The boundary between Canada and the USA is mostly at exactly 49°N. Four of the five Great Lakes have one shore in Canada and one shore in the USA★. Canada's two biggest cities, Toronto and Montreal, are south of the 49° line! Find them on the map on page 65.

The eight countries of Central America have more complicated boundaries. Six of these countries have two coastlines. The map shows that one country has a coastline only on the Pacific Ocean, and one has a coastline only on the Caribbean Sea★. The West Indies are made up of islands and there are lots of countries too. They are shown in more detail on pages 74 and 75.

Greenland used to be a colony of Denmark, but now it is self-governing. Most of Greenland is covered by ice all year.

★Which ones? Answers on page 96.

Fact box: North America

Area 24,249,000 square kilometres
Highest point Mount McKinley (Alaska), 6194 metres
Lowest point Death Valley (California), 86 metres below sea-level
Longest river Red Rock–Missouri–Mississippi, 5970 kilometres
Largest lake Lake Superior★, 82,350 square kilometres
Biggest country Canada, 9,976,140 square kilometres
Smallest country Grenada (West Indies), 344 square kilometres
Richest country USA
Poorest country Haiti
Most crowded country Barbados
Least crowded country Canada

★The world's largest *freshwater* lake

▼ *Flyovers, Los Angeles, USA.*
There are four levels of road at this road junction in Los Angeles, yet there is a traffic-jam as well! In 1994, a huge earthquake destroyed many road bridges.

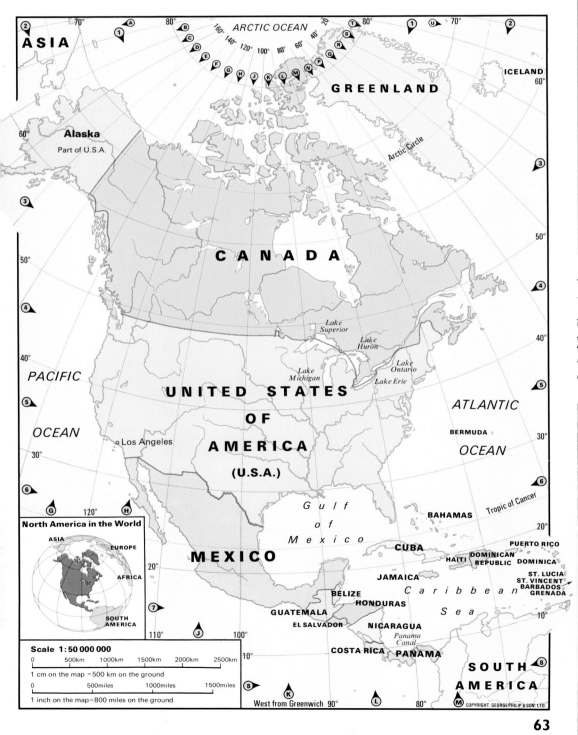

ARCTIC OCEAN

ASIA

ICELAND

GREENLAND

Alaska
Part of U.S.A.

Arctic Circle

C A N A D A

PACIFIC

OCEAN

Lake Superior
Lake Huron
Lake Michigan
Lake Ontario
Lake Erie

U N I T E D   S T A T E S

O F

A M E R I C A

(U.S.A.)

Los Angeles

ATLANTIC

OCEAN

BERMUDA

Tropic of Cancer

Gulf
of
Mexico

M E X I C O

BAHAMAS

CUBA
HAITI   DOMINICAN REPUBLIC   DOMINICA
PUERTO RICO
JAMAICA
ST. LUCIA
ST. VINCENT
BARBADOS
GRENADA

BELIZE
HONDURAS
GUATEMALA
EL SALVADOR   NICARAGUA
Panama Canal
COSTA RICA   PANAMA

Caribbean
Sea

SOUTH
AMERICA

West from Greenwich 90°

North America in the World

ASIA   EUROPE

AFRICA

SOUTH
AMERICA

Scale 1:50 000 000

| 0 | 500km | 1000km | 1500km | 2000km | 2500km |

1 cm on the map = 500 km on the ground

| 0 | 500miles | 1000miles | 1500miles |

1 inch on the map = 800 miles on the ground

COPYRIGHT. GEORGE PHILIP & SON. LTD.

CANADA

▲ **Coin and flag.** *Both the 1 cent coin and the flag show the national emblem of Canada, the maple leaf. In summer, the leaves of the maple tree are green, but in the fall (autumn) the leaves turn bright red. Canada's woodlands are especially beautiful in September and October (see photograph below right).*

Canadian contrasts

▲ This stamp is an air-picture of the prairies of central Canada. The huge flat fields of grain reach to the far horizon, and beyond. The only big buildings are grain elevators, for storing the harvested wheat.

▼ In western Canada, the Rocky Mountains are high and jagged. There are glaciers among the peaks.

Only one country in the world is bigger than Canada★, but 30 countries have more people than Canada. Most of Canada is almost empty: very few people live on the islands of the north, or in the Northwest Territories, or in the western mountains, or near Hudson Bay. The farmland of the prairies (see the stamp) is uncrowded too. So … where *do* Canadians live?

The answer is that more Canadians live in cities than in the countryside. The map shows where the biggest cities are – all of them are in the southern part of Canada, and none are as far north as Norway or Sweden in Europe.

The photographs and stamps show Canada in summer. In winter, it is very cold indeed in both central and northern Canada. Children go to school even when it is 40° below zero.

★Which country? See page 9.

▲ **The Niagara Falls** *are between Lake Erie and Lake Ontario, on the border of the USA and Canada. The tourists on the boat may get soaked by the spray! Big ships have to use a canal, with locks, to get past the falls.*

Languages in Canada

Canada has two official languages: French and English. So the stamps say 'Postes/Postage', instead of only 'Postage'. Most of the French-speaking Canadians live in the province of Quebec.

The biggest city in Quebec is Montreal: it is four times as big as Ottawa, the capital of Canada.

▼ **A long-distance train,** *with diesel engines and silver coaches, crosses a viaduct in the province of Ontario. It is 4590 kilometres from Montreal to Vancouver by train. A hundred years ago it was the trans-Canada railway that helped to unite Canada as one country.*

How to remember the five Great Lakes

Try using the first letters of the Great Lakes to make a sentence:

Superior	**S**uper
Michigan	**M**an
Huron	**H**elps
Erie	**E**very
Ontario	**O**ne

Now you'll *never* forget the west-to-east order of the Great Lakes!

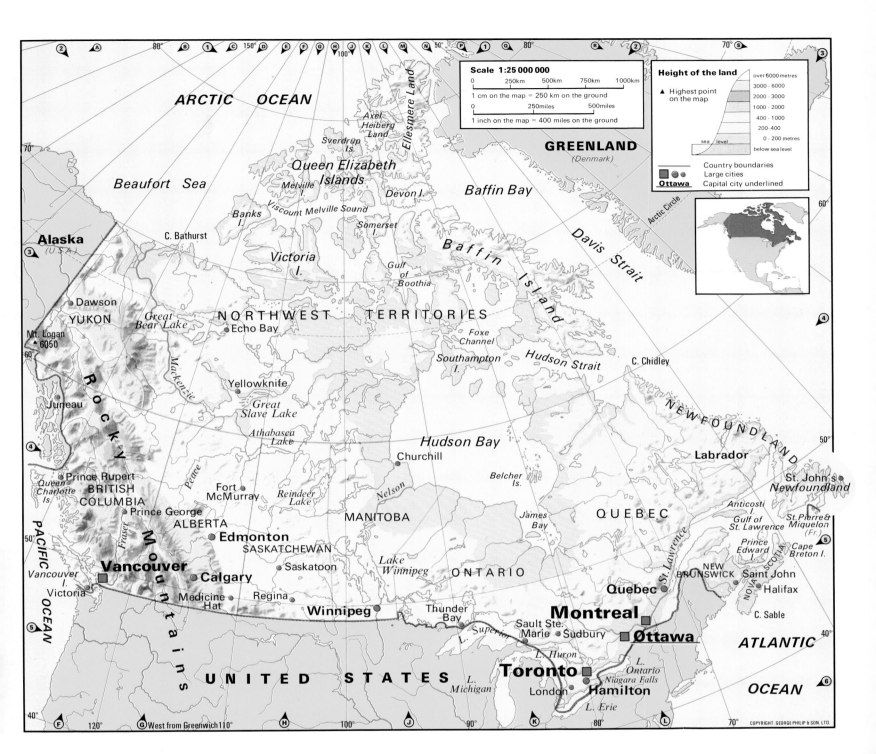

ARCTIC OCEAN

Scale 1:25 000 000

0	250km	500km	750km	1000km

1 cm on the map = 250 km on the ground

0	250miles	500miles

1 inch on the map = 400 miles on the ground

Height of the land

▲ Highest point on the map	over 6000 metres
	3000 - 6000
	2000 - 3000
	1000 - 2000
	400 - 1000
	200 - 400
sea level	0 - 200 metres
	below sea level

Country boundaries
Large cities
Ottawa Capital city underlined

Axel Heiberg Land

Sverdrup Is.

Ellesmere Land

GREENLAND
(Denmark)

Queen Elizabeth Islands

Beaufort Sea

Melville I.

Devon I.

Baffin Bay

Banks I.

Viscount Melville Sound

Somerset I.

Baffin Island

Davis Strait

Arctic Circle

C. Bathurst

Victoria I.

Gulf of Boothia

Alaska
(U.S.A.)

Dawson

YUKON

Great Bear Lake

NORTHWEST   TERRITORIES

Foxe Channel

C. Chidley

Mt. Logan
▲ 6050

Echo Bay

Southampton I.

Hudson Strait

NEWFOUNDLAND

Juneau

Mackenzie

Yellowknife

Great Slave Lake

Hudson Bay

Labrador

Athabasca Lake

Churchill

Belcher Is.

St. John's
Newfoundland

Prince Rupert

BRITISH COLUMBIA

Queen Charlotte Is.

Fort McMurray

Reindeer Lake

Nelson

James Bay

QUEBEC

Anticosti I.

Gulf of St. Lawrence

St. Pierre & Miquelon (Fr.)

Prince George

ALBERTA

MANITOBA

Prince Edward I.

Cape Breton I.

Edmonton

SASKATCHEWAN

Lake Winnipeg

ONTARIO

St. Lawrence

NEW BRUNSWICK

Saint John

Vancouver

Calgary

Saskatoon

Quebec

NOVA SCOTIA

Halifax

PACIFIC OCEAN

Vancouver I.

Victoria

Medicine Hat

Regina

Winnipeg

Thunder Bay

L. Superior

Sault Ste. Marie

Sudbury

Montreal

Ottawa

C. Sable

ATLANTIC

Rocky Mountains

Fraser

Peace

L. Huron

Toronto

L. Ontario
Niagara Falls

Hamilton

OCEAN

UNITED   STATES

London

L. Michigan

L. Erie

West from Greenwich

COPYRIGHT. GEORGE PHILIP & SON. LTD.

◀ **Montreal: old and new.**
Some of the old houses have been pulled down, to make way for huge new office blocks. Three million people live in Montreal.

▶ **The St Lawrence.** This big ship is passing islands in the St Lawrence River. The ship is going from the Great Lakes to the Atlantic Ocean. A seaway with huge locks has been built to bypass the rapids, shallows and waterfalls on parts of the river.

USA

Alaska is the biggest state of the USA – but it has the fewest people. It was bought from Russia in 1867 for $7 million: the best bargain ever, particularly as oil was discovered a hundred years later. Oil has helped Alaska to become rich. Timber and fish are the other main products.

Much of Alaska is mountainous or covered in forest. In the north, there is darkness all day in December, and months of ice-cold weather.

The Flag of Alaska shows stars in the northern sky known as the 'plough' or 'the big dipper'. At the top right is the Pole Star. The flag was chosen in a competition; the winner was only 13 years old.

These are 48 of the 50 states. The other two are Alaska (map above) and Hawaii (map below).
⭐ State capital

ABBREVIATIONS
VT. = Vermont
N.H. = New Hampshire
MASS. = Massachusetts
CONN. = Connecticut
D.C. = District of Columbia

Hawaii is the newest state in the USA: it became a state in 1959. Honolulu is on Oahu island.

These faraway Pacific islands are the tops of volcanoes, over 3000 kilometres from mainland USA (see map page 83). If the height of Mauna Kea is measured from the sea-bed, it is 10,023 metres: the world's highest mountain.

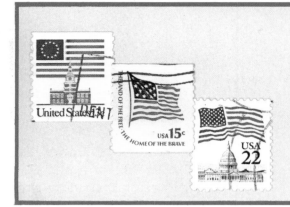

The Stars and Stripes

In 1776 there were only 13 states in the USA: so the US flag had 13 stars and 13 stripes. As more and more states joined the USA, more stars were added to the flag. Now there are 50 states, and 50 stars. But the 13 stripes on today's flag still recall the original 13 states.

The maps show the 50 states of the USA. The first 13 states were all on the east coast: these states were settled by Europeans who had sailed across the Atlantic (see the photograph of a pilgrim ship on page 69).

As the Americans moved westwards, so more and more states were formed. The western states are bigger than the states in the east. You can see their straight boundaries on the map.

Who are 'the Americans'?

Out of every 100 people in the USA, 83 have ancestors from Europe. Colonists came from Britain to the eastern states, from France to the southern states, and from Spain to the Pacific coast in the west. Later on, people came from almost all parts of Europe to the USA. About 12 people out of every 100 came from West Africa, brought to the USA as slaves to work in the southern states. By 1865, the slaves were free. Many black Americans now live in the north-east USA. More recently, many Spanish-speaking people have entered the USA from Mexico and from Puerto Rico.

There are fewer than one million American Indians now, some of whom live on special 'reservations'.

▲ **5 cent coin.** E PLURIBUS UNUM *on this coin is Latin for 'Out of many — one': many peoples have come together to become one country. This 5 cent coin is called a nickel.*

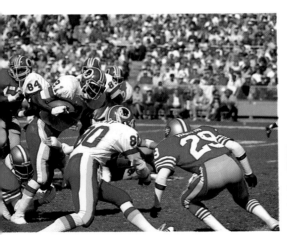

▲ **American football.** *The Washington Redskins play the San Francisco 49ers. The team from the west coast has travelled 4500 kilometres for this game. The players travel by air — it takes three days to cross the USA by train!*

▼ **State flags.** *Each state has its own flag and some of them tell you about the history of the state.*

▲ **Wyoming** *has a buffalo in the centre of its flag because this state was part of the Wild West where buffaloes used to roam freely.*

▲ **Mississippi** *has the French flag (red, white and blue stripes) because it belonged to France until 1803. The cross at top left was used as a flag by the southern states in the Civil War in 1861–5.*

Distance chart

	New York	Miami	Chicago	New Orleans	Seattle
Miami	2138				
Chicago	1346	2198			
New Orleans	2131	1406	1488		
Seattle	4613	5445	3288	4211	
San Francisco	4850	4915	3499	3622	1352

Road distances in kilometres

Read the chart just like a tables-chart, or a graph. The distance chart shows how big the USA is. In fact, New York is nearer to London, England, than it is to San Francisco! How far is it from Seattle to Miami? New Orleans to Chicago?

Find these places on the maps on pages 68-71.(Answers on page 96.)

EASTERN USA

Which US city is most important?

Washington is the capital city, where the President lives. But *New York* has far more people and industries than Washington. So *both* are the most important city – but in different ways.

The map shows only half the USA, but over three-quarters of the population live in this half of the country.

The great cities of the north-east were the first big industrial areas in America. Pittsburgh's American football team is still called the Pittsburgh Steelers, even though many of the steelworks have closed down.

In recent years, many people have moved from the 'snow-belt' of the north to the 'sun-belt' of the south. New industries are booming in the south, where once there was much poverty. And many older people retire to Florida, where even mid-winter feels almost like summer.

In the south of the USA it is hot enough for cotton, tobacco and peanuts to be successful crops.

The Appalachian Mountains are beautiful, especially in the fall (autumn), when the leaves of the trees turn red. But this area is the poorest part of the USA. Coal mines have closed and farmland is poor. The good farmland is west of the Appalachians, where you can drive for hundreds of kilometres past wheat and sweetcorn.

Plan for better cities!

Turn the book clockwise and you will see patios, parks and gardens among the skyscrapers!

▲ *Washington, DC.* ▶
There is a world of difference between the well-kept rich suburbs (above) and the run-down slum area (right) of Washington, DC. (DC = District of Colombia).

▼ *Manhattan Island, New York.*
The world's first skyscrapers were built on Manhattan Island: the hard granite rock gave good foundations. The older skyscrapers each have a different shape; the newer ones are flat-topped.

▲ **Plantation-owner's house in Virginia.** *Plantation owners grew rich from tobacco and cotton. They lived in fine houses like this one. But their slaves lived in very poor houses.*

◄ **Winter in Pittsburgh.** *Winter in the northern USA can be very cold indeed. But these Pittsburgh children are enjoying the fresh, crisp snow, before it becomes polluted by smoke from the steelworks and factories.*

The Earth from the Moon

This is the view that American astronauts saw from the Moon. Half the Earth is in darkness. Neil Armstrong of the USA was the first man on the Moon, 21 July 1969.

▲ **Pilgrim ship, New England.** *The Pilgrim Fathers sailed to America in 1620 from England to start a new life. In 1957 a replica pilgrim ship was built and sailed to America.*

Puzzle stamp

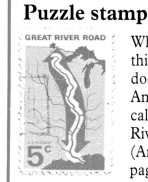

Which river is this? Where does it flow to? And why is it called 'Great River Road'? (Answer on page 96.)

Map

Scale 1:20 000 000

| 0 | 200km | 400km | 600km | 800km |

1 cm on the map = 200 km on the ground

| 0 | 200miles | 400miles |

1 inch on the map = 320 miles on the ground

Height of the land

▲ Highest point on the map

over 6000 metres
4000 - 6000
2000 - 4000
1000 - 2000
400 - 1000
200 - 400
0 - 200 metres
below sea level

sea level

Country boundaries
Large cities
Washington Capital city underlined
For the states of the U.S.A. see page 66

CANADA

Fargo
Duluth
Minneapolis
St. Paul
Sioux Falls
Milwaukee
Chicago
Detroit
Toledo
Cleveland
Pittsburgh
Omaha
Indianapolis
Columbus
Kansas City
Cincinnati
Ohio
Wichita
St. Louis
Louisville
Richmond
Norfolk
Tulsa
Nashville
Mt. Mitchell 2037
Charlotte
Oklahoma City
Memphis
Chattanooga
Atlanta
Birmingham
Charleston
Fort Worth
Dallas
Montgomery
Jacksonville
Austin
Baton Rouge
Houston
New Orleans
San Antonio
Tampa
Palm Beach
Gulf of Mexico
Miami
C. Sable
Key West

Boston
Albany
Buffalo
Providence
C. Cod
New York
Philadelphia
Baltimore
Washington
ATLANTIC OCEAN
C. Canaveral
BAHAMAS

Lake Superior
Lake Michigan
Lake Huron
L. Ontario
Lake Erie
Hudson
Mississippi
Missouri
Arkansas
Red
Tennessee
Appalachian Mts.
Everglades

West from Greenwich

COPYRIGHT GEORGE PHILIP & SON. LTD.

WESTERN USA

▲ Grand Canyon, Arizona.
The Colorado River has cut a huge
canyon a mile deep in this desert
area of the USA. The mountains
slowly rose, while the river kept
digging its valley deeper.

▼ Wheat harvest, USA. Three
huge combine harvesters move
across a field of wheat. 150 years
ago, this land was covered in grass
and grazed by buffaloes. Much of
this wheat will go abroad.

American football

Many of the team names have a
meaning that is linked to their
city's geography or history.

San Francisco 49ers: 1849 was
the year of the great Californian
Gold Rush, when many people
came to look for gold.

Denver Broncos: Denver,
Colorado, was a centre for cowboys
in the days of the Wild West;
'bucking broncos' were their horses!

Houston Oilers: Houston, Texas,
became a very wealthy city after
oil was discovered.

Seattle Seahawks: Seattle,
Washington State, is on an inlet
of the Pacific Ocean.

Do you know any other teams?

▲ Rodeo in Montana. There are
few real cowboys nowadays – and
trucks are used more than horses.
But rodeos are popular with local
people – and with tourists. At this
junior rodeo at Big Timber, Montana,
a young rider is trying to show his
skill.

California

California now has more people in
it than any other state in the USA.
It has every advantage. In the
Central Valley the climate is right
for many crops: oranges from
California are well known in the
USA and abroad. Grapes grow
well, and are made into wine.

The desert of the south is
attractive to retired people –
many people migrate here from
all over the USA.

Many areas on this map have hardly any people. The Rocky Mountains are beautiful for holidays, but it is hard to make a living there. The only big city on the high plateaus west of the Rockies is Salt Lake City, Utah. Some former mining towns are now 'ghost towns': when the mines closed, all the people left. The toughest area of all is the desert land of Arizona in the south-west. The mountains and deserts were a great problem to the pioneers.

East of the Rockies are the Great Plains. The dry plains have enormous cattle ranches; where there is enough rain, crops of wheat and sweetcorn (maize) stretch to the horizon.

The Pacific coastlands of the north-west have plenty of rain and forestry is important. The climate is quite like north-west Europe.

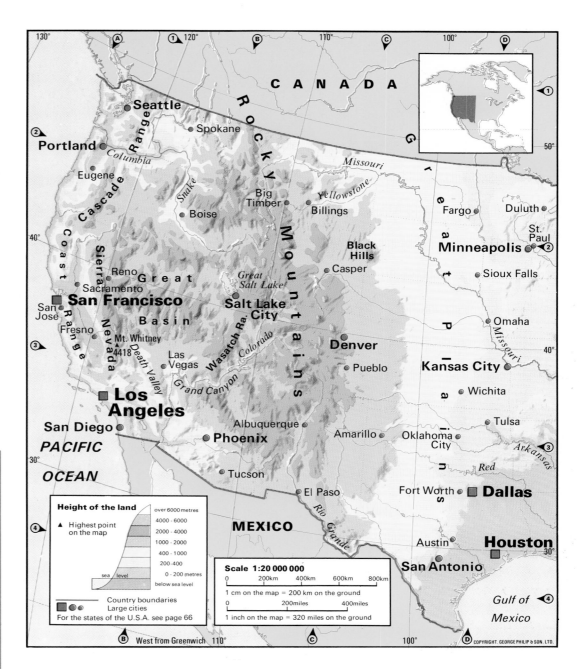

What do the names mean?

The Spanish were the first settlers in the western USA, and they have left us many Spanish names. Here are some:

Amarillo (Texas) .... Yellow
Colorado .... Coloured
El Paso (Texas) .... The pass
Los Angeles .... The angels
Las Vegas (Nevada).... The fertile
                              plains
San José .... St Joseph
San Francisco .... St Francis
Sierra Nevada .... Snowy
                              Mountains

▶ *Street-car, San Francisco.*
Street-cars still climb the steep hills in San Francisco, California. A moving cable runs beneath the street. The car is fixed to the cable and starts with a jerk! There is a modern 'rapid transit' railway system too — but tourists prefer to see the city from the street-cars.

CENTRAL AMERICA

◄ **Ruins at Chichen Itza, Mexico.** *Great temples were built by the people known as Mayas over a thousand years ago. These amazing ruins are in Yucatan, the most easterly part of Mexico. Today, this is an area of jungle, with few people.*

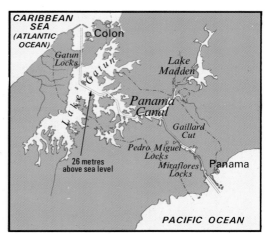

The Panama Canal links the Caribbean Sea with the Pacific Ocean. It was opened in 1914. Many workers died of fever while digging the canal through the jungle. It is 82 kilometres long, and the deepest cutting is 82 metres deep – the world's biggest 'ditch'!

There are six locks along the route of the canal. The photograph (below left) shows three ships in Gatun Lake, 26 metres above sea-level (see map). Over 15,000 ships use the canal each year, and sometimes there are 'traffic jams' at the locks: it is the busiest big ship canal in the world. Before the Panama Canal was built, the only sea route from Pacific to Atlantic was round South America.

MEXICAN TORTILLAS

A recipe for you to cook

Ingredients
225 grams of maize flour
(sweetcorn flour)
salt
water

Method
1 Mix the maize flour, salt and water into a soft dough.
2 Pat into round shapes about ½ centimetre thick, and 12 centimetres across.
3 Melt a little margarine in a frying-pan.
4 Place the tortillas in the hot frying-pan.
5 For best results, turn the tortillas over.
6 Serve at once!

You have now cooked one of the most important meals of Central America. Maize (sweetcorn) was developed as a crop in the Americas, and is now grown in many parts of the world. You eat maize often as Corn Flakes and semolina.

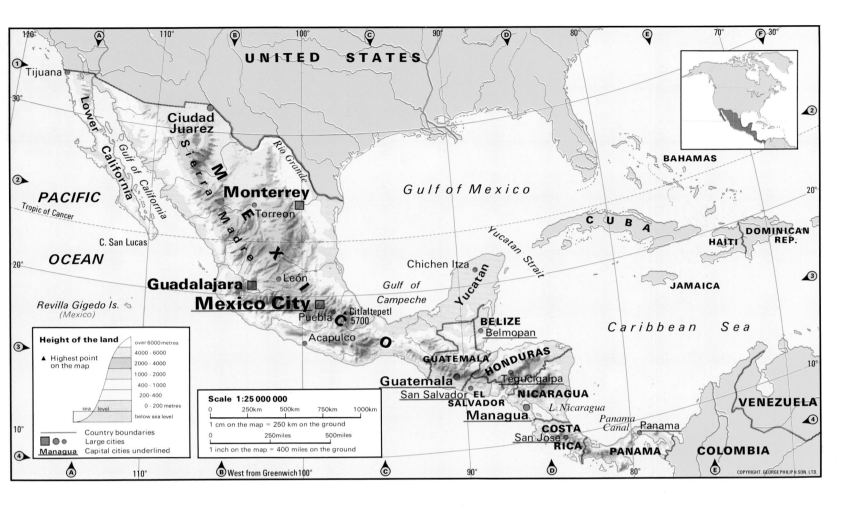

Mexico is by far the most important country on this map. Over 82 million people live in Mexico – more than in any country in Europe. Mexico City has a population of about 15 million: it is one of the biggest cities in the world. A major earthquake did much damage there in 1985.

Most Mexicans live on the high plateau of central Mexico. There are very few people in the northern desert, in Lower California in the north-west, in the southern jungle, or in Yucatan in the east.

The other seven countries on this map are quite small. None of them has as many people as Mexico City!

Once ruled by Spain, these countries have been independent since the 1820s. Revolutions and civil wars have caused many problems in Central America. But the climate is good for growing many tropical crops – once the jungle has been cleared.

What do the names mean?

Many names in the countries of Central America are based on Spanish, the official language.

El Salvador The Saviour (Jesus Christ)
San José St Joseph (capital of Costa Rica)
Costa Rica The rich coast
Pacific Ocean Peaceful ocean

▼ **Guatemala: drying coffee-beans.** *Coffee berries grow on bushes in tropical countries. The berries are picked, and the seeds taken out and dried in the sun. We call these dried seeds coffee-beans.*

The man in the photograph is turning the beans, so that they dry on both sides.

Coffee is the most important export of several Central American countries. Many other tropical crops are exported, including sugar, bananas and pineapple.

WEST INDIES

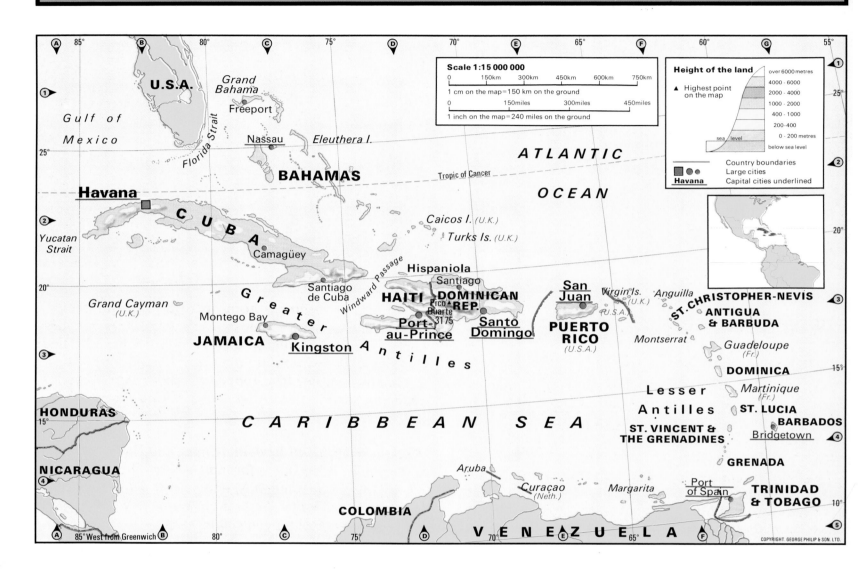

Farming in Jamaica

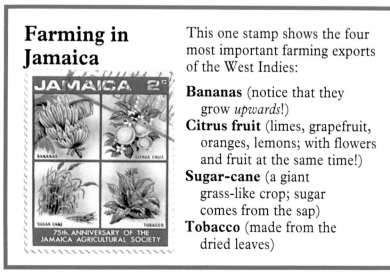

This one stamp shows the four most important farming exports of the West Indies:

Bananas (notice that they grow *upwards!*)

Citrus fruit (limes, grapefruit, oranges, lemons; with flowers and fruit at the same time!)

Sugar-cane (a giant grass-like crop; sugar comes from the sap)

Tobacco (made from the dried leaves)

The West Indies are a large group of islands in the Caribbean Sea. Some islands are high and volcanic, others are low coral islands – but all of them are beautiful. Most West Indians have African ancestors: they were brought from West Africa as slaves, to work in the sugar and tobacco fields.

Today, most of the islands are independent countries – and tourism is more important than farming in many places. Winter is the best time to visit; summer is very hot and humid, with the risk of hurricanes. In recent years many West Indians have emigrated to the UK from Commonwealth islands, to France from Guadeloupe and Martinique, and to the USA from Puerto Rico. A few islands have developed their minerals, for example bauxite in Jamaica and oil in Trinidad.

◀ *Coconut-palms and beach, Barbados.* It is beautiful – but beware! The tropical sun can quickly burn your skin. And if you seek shade under the coconut-palms, you might get hit by a big coconut! Even so, the West Indies are very popular with tourists – especially Americans escaping from cold winters.

West Indian variety

◀ In **Cuba**, Spanish is the main language. Cuba is the biggest West Indian island, and the nearest to the USA.

▶ **St Vincent** is part of the Commonwealth and seems very British (but arrowroot and breadfruit only grow in the tropics).

◀ **Guadeloupe** is not just French – it is officially part of France. This stamp was used in Guadeloupe *and* in all of France!

▶ **Curaçao** is Dutch: the stamp shows Dutch colonial houses, and the Queen of the Netherlands. Compare the photograph (right).

▲ *Loading bananas, Dominica.* Bananas are the main export of several islands. Here women are carrying heavy loads of bananas on their heads to the small boats which take the bananas to the Geest banana ship. The bananas travel to Europe in this refrigerated ship. Loading the ship is easier where islands have deep-water harbours.

▼ *Dutch colonial houses, Curaçao.* The island of Curaçao has been Dutch for many years. The colonists came from the Netherlands, and tried to build houses just like the ones at home. Several other small West Indian islands still have European connections.

SOUTH AMERICA

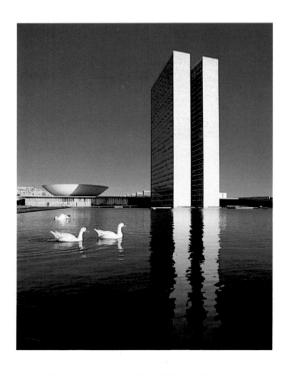

◀ **Brasilia, Brazil.** *Brasilia became the new capital of Brazil in 1960. The photograph shows the parliament building on the left, built in concrete and shaped like a bowl, and a tall office block. Most Brazilians live near the coast, and Brasilia was a brave attempt to get people to move inland: it is 1000 kilometres from the sea. Over a million people now live there.*

Fact box: South America

Area 17,600,000 square kilometres

Highest point Mount Aconcagua (Argentina), 6960 metres

Lowest point No land below sea-level

Longest river Amazon, 6448 kilometres

Largest lake Lake Titicaca (Bolivia and Peru), 8285 square kilometres

Biggest country Brazil, 8,511,965 square kilometres

Smallest country Surinam★, 163,265 square kilometres

Richest country Venezuela

Poorest country Bolivia

Most crowded country Ecuador

Least crowded country Surinam

★French Guiana is smaller, but it is not independent

◀ **Reed-boat on Lake Titicaca.**
Lake Titicaca is the highest navigable
lake in the world: 3811 metres above
sea-level. The fishing-boat is made of
totora reeds which grow around the
shores. Bundles of reeds are tied
together, and even the sails are
made of woven reeds.

The lake is shared between Peru
and Bolivia. A steam-powered ferry-
boat travels the length of the lake.
A river flows southwards from Lake
Titicaca to Lake Poopo.

Why is Lake Titicaca the only
stretch of water available to the
Bolivian navy? (Check the map.)

A tour of South America would be
very exciting. At the Equator are the
hot steamy jungles of the Amazon
lowlands. To the west comes the
great climb up to the Andes
Mountains. The peaks are so high that
even the volcanoes are snow-capped
all year. Travellers on buses and trains
are offered extra oxygen to breathe,
because the air is so thin.

Squeezed between the Andes and
the Pacific Ocean in Peru and northern Chile is the world's driest desert.
Further south in Chile are more wet
forests – but these forests are cool.
The Chilean pine (monkey-puzzle
tree) originates here. But eastwards,
in Argentina, there is less rain and
more grass. Cattle on the Pampas are
rounded up by cowboys, and further
south is the very cold and dry area
called Patagonia.

South America stretches further
south than any other continent (apart
from Antarctica). The cold and
stormy tip of South America, Cape
Horn, is only 1000 kilometres from
Antarctica.

In every South American country,
the population is growing fast. Most
of the farmland is owned by a few
rich people, and many people are
desperately poor. Young people are
leaving the countryside for the cities,
most of which are encircled by shanty
towns.

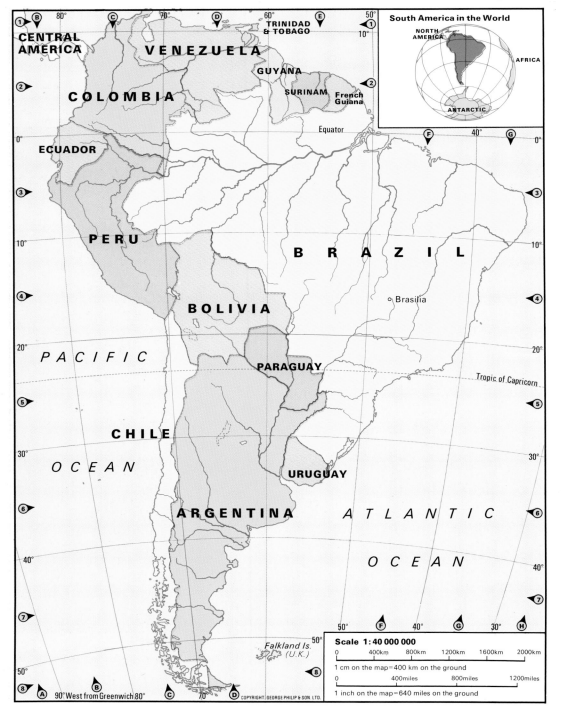

South America in the World

Scale 1:40 000 000

| 0 | 400km | 800km | 1200km | 1600km | 2000km |

1 cm on the map = 400 km on the ground

| 0 | 400miles | 800miles | 1200miles |

1 inch on the map = 640 miles on the ground

COPYRIGHT. GEORGE PHILIP & SON. LTD.

TROPICAL SOUTH AMERICA

▲ **Amazon jungle** at the border of Guyana and Brazil. The hot, wet jungle covers thousands of kilometres. There is no cool season, and the forest is always green. The trees can be 50 metres high. New roads and villages, mines and dams are being built in the Brazilian jungle, and parts of the forest are being destroyed.

The Andean states.

Colombia, Ecuador, Peru and Bolivia are known as the Andean states. **Colombia** is known for its coffee. Bananas and other tropical crops grow near the coast of **Ecuador**, but the capital city is high in the mountains. **Peru** relies on mountain rivers to bring water to the dry coastal area. **Bolivia** has the highest capital city in the world. It is the poorest country in South America: farming is difficult and even the tin mines hardly make a profit.

East of the Andes, settlers are clearing parts of the forest.

▼ **Machu Picchu, Peru,** the lost city of the Incas, is perched on a mountainside 2400 metres above sea-level. The last Inca emperor probably lived here in 1580. The ruins were rediscovered in 1911.

Brazil – the giant.

Brazil is by far the biggest country in South America, and has more people (about 151 million) than the rest of South America put together.

Most people still live near the coast. Parts of the Amazon forest are now being settled, but large areas inland are still almost empty. The poorest parts are in the north-east, where the rains often fail, and in the shanty towns around the big cities. Modern industry is growing very fast, but there are still too few jobs. Brazil has pioneered fuel made from sugarcane for cars and trucks.

▼ **The llama** is the most important animal in the Andes – it provides milk, meat and leather for these Quechua Indian women. They are following one of the Inca tracks which linked the ancient cities.

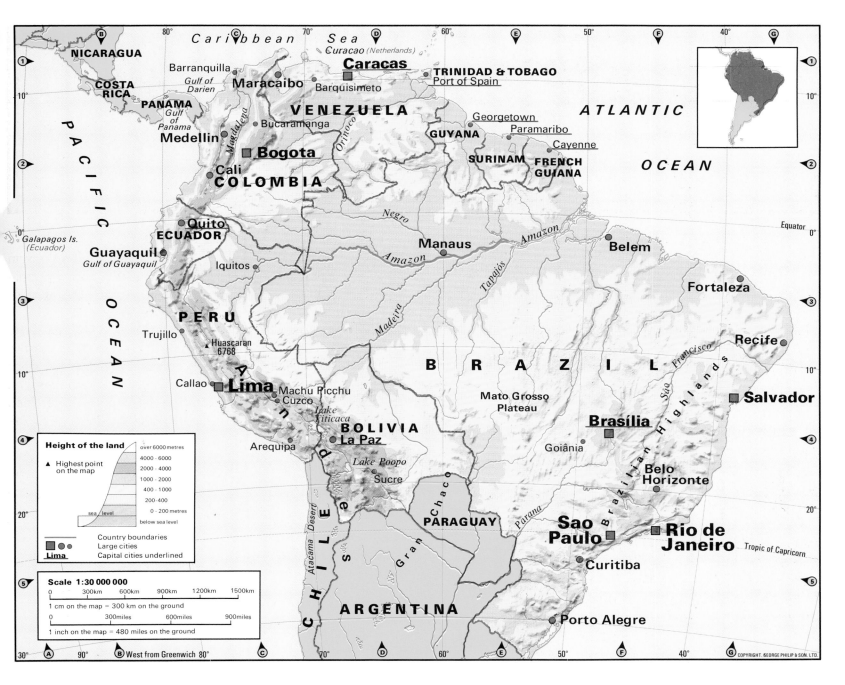

Height of the land

	over 6000 metres
▲ Highest point on the map	4000 - 6000
	2000 - 4000
	1000 - 2000
	400 - 1000
	200 - 400
sea level	0 - 200 metres
	below sea level

■ Country boundaries
●● Large cities
Lima Capital cities underlined

Scale 1:30 000 000

0	300km	600km	900km	1200km	1500km

1 cm on the map = 300 km on the ground

0	300miles	600miles	900miles

1 inch on the map = 480 miles on the ground

▶ **Cattle and cowboys.** *To the south of the Amazon jungle, there is a large area of dry woodland and grassland in Brazil called the Mato Grosso. Cattle are grazed here, and horses are still used to round them up.*

Did you know?

Ecuador means *Equator*: the Equator (0°) crosses the country.

Colombia is named after Christopher *Columbus*, who sailed from Europe to the Americas in 1492.

Bolivia is named after Simon *Bolivar*, a hero of the country's war of independence in the 1820s.

La Paz, the biggest town in Bolivia, means *peace*. But there have been over 100 revolutions in Bolivia, the highest total in the world!

TEMPERATE SOUTH AMERICA

Chile is 4300 kilometres long, but it is only about 200 kilometres wide, because it is sandwiched between the Andes and the Pacific. In the *north* is the Atacama Desert, the driest in the world. In one place, there was no rain for 400 years! Fortunately, rivers from the Andes permit some irrigation. Chilean nitrates come from this area. Nitrates are salts in dried-up lakes; they are used to make fertilizers and explosives. Copper is mined high in the mountains and is Chile's main export.

In the *centre*, the climate is like the Mediterranean area and California, with hot dry summers and warm wet winters with westerly winds (six words begin with W: it's easy to remember!) This is a lovely climate, and most Chileans live in this area.

In the *south*, Chile is wet, windy and cool. Thick forests which include the Chilean pine (monkey-puzzle tree) cover the steep hills. The reason for these contrasts is the wind. Winds bringing cloud and rain blow from the Pacific Ocean all year in the south; but only in winter in the centre; and not at all in the north.

▲ **Geysers in the Andes, Chile.** *Hot steam hisses into the cold air, 4000 metres above sea-level in the Andes of northern Chile.*

The Falkland Islands

These islands are a British colony in the South Atlantic. They are about 480 kilometres east of Argentina, which claims them as the Islas Malvinas. Britain fought an Argentine invasion in 1982, and the military force is now as large as the population (only 2000). Sheep farming is the main occupation.

◄ The capital city, Port Stanley, has houses that look quite like English houses, but the remote farmhouses get their post by 'mail drop' from a Beaver aircraft (see stamp above right). Until recently, there were no roads to these farms.

► This stamp shows Argentina's claim that the Falkland Islands are part of Argentina.

The Andes

The Andes are over 7000 kilometres long, so they are the longest mountain range in the world. They are fold mountains, with a very steep western side, and a gentler eastern side. Most of the high peaks are volcanoes: they are the highest volcanoes in the world. Mount Aconcagua (6960 metres) is an extinct volcano. Mount Guallatiri, in Chile, is the world's highest active volcano – it last erupted in 1969.

The higher you climb, the cooler it is. And the further you travel from the Equator, the cooler it is. Therefore, the snowline in southern Chile is *much* lower than in northern Chile.

Argentina means 'silvery' in Spanish: some of the early settlers came to mine silver. But today, Argentina's most important product is cattle. Cool grasslands called the Pampas are ideal for cattle-grazing.

Argentina is a varied country: the north-west is hot and dry, and the south is cold and dry (see photograph). The frontier with Chile runs high along the top of the Andes.

Buenos Aires, the capital city, is the biggest city in South America; it has 10 million people. The name means 'good air', but petrol fumes have now polluted the air.

Paraguay and **Uruguay** are two countries with small populations. Each country has under five million people. Nearly half the population of Uruguay lives in the capital city, Montevideo, which is on the coast. In contrast Paraguay is completely land-locked. Animal farming is the most important occupation in both these countries.

▼ **Sheep farming in Patagonia, Argentina.** *Southern Argentina has a cool, dry climate. Very few people live there – but lots of sheep roam the extensive grasslands. There are almost as many sheep in Argentina as there are people.*

THE PACIFIC

This map shows half the world. Guess which place is furthest from a continent: it is somewhere in the South Pacific. The Pacific also includes the deepest place in the world: the Mariana Trench (11,022 metres deep). It would take over an hour for a steel ball weighing half a kilogram to fall to the bottom!

There are thousands of islands in the Pacific Ocean. Some are volcanic mountains, while many others are low, flat coral islands. Coral also grows around the volcanoes (see photograph below).

A few islands have valuable minerals – for example Nauru (phosphates) and Bougainville (copper). But most islanders are occupied in farming. Many tropical crops grow well; sugar-cane, bananas and pineapples are important exports. Islands big enough for a full-sized airport, such as Fiji, the Samoan islands, Tahiti, and Hawaii (see page 66), now get many globe-trotting tourists.

▼ **Moorea from the air.** The coral reef can be clearly seen around this island in French Polynesia; the reef makes it difficult for ships to reach the land.

The island is steep and rugged: it is an old volcano. Notice the deep valleys dug by rivers. The white patches are clouds, not snow.

▶ **Easter Island, South Pacific.** *These huge stone sculptures each weigh about 50 tonnes! They were cut long ago with simple stone axes, and lifted with ropes and ramps – an amazing achievement for people who had no metal, no wheels and no machines.*

Look for Easter Island on the map (in square U 11): it is one of the remotest places in the world. It is now owned by Chile, 3860 kilometres away in South America.

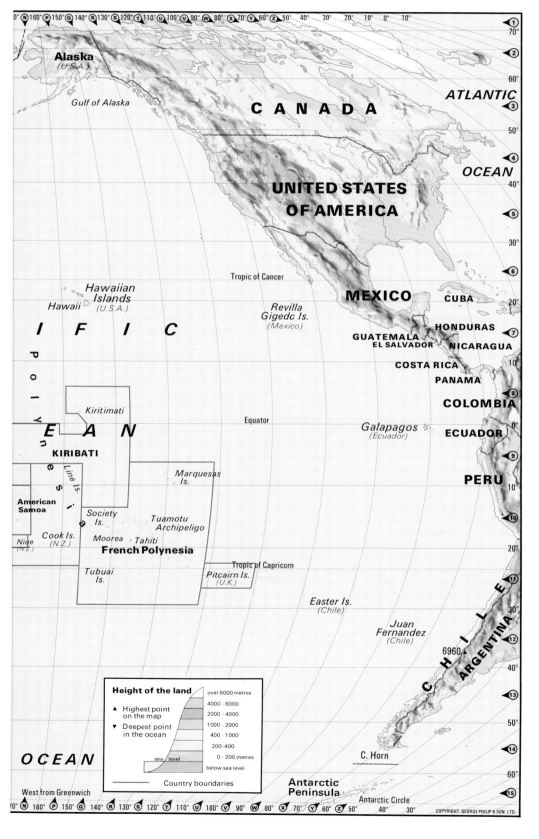

Most Pacific countries are large groups of small islands. Their boundaries are out at sea – just lines on a map. Kiribati is 33 small coral atolls spread over 5 million square kilometres of ocean. And the Solomon Islands stretch for 1450 kilometres. Imagine organizing something for the whole country!

Pacific stamps

The stamp from **French Polynesia** shows coconut-palms and an outrigger canoe: you can see how this makes the dug-out canoe more stable at sea. In the background, there are canoes with sails.

In the highlands of **Papua New Guinea** (north of Australia), people live in round huts with thatched roofs. The stamp also shows the island's high, rugged mountains.

AUSTRALIA

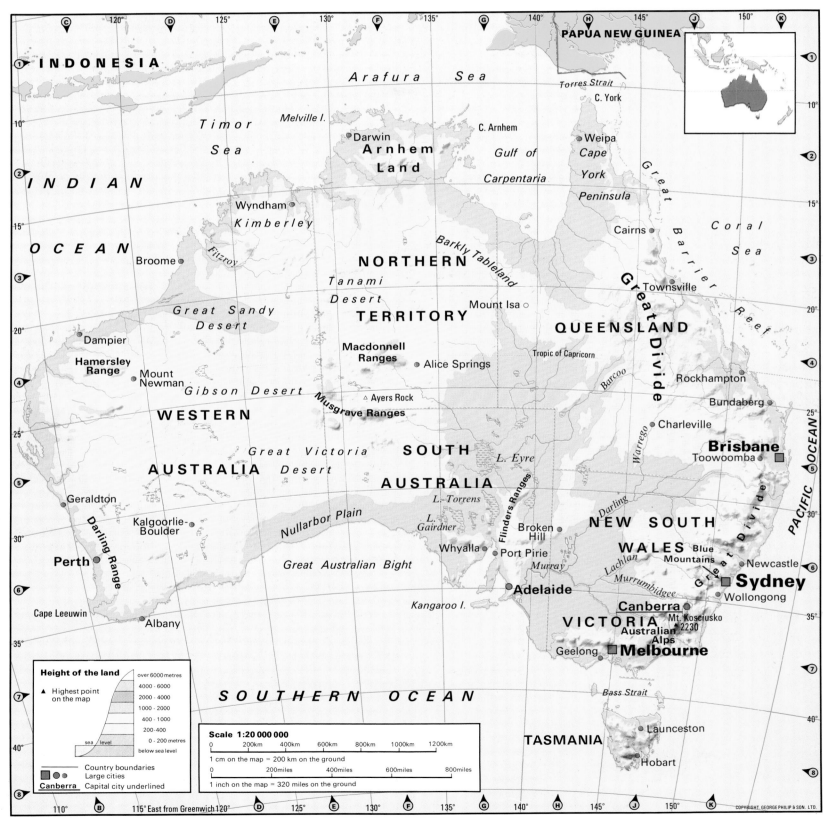

INDONESIA

Arafura Sea

Torres Strait

PAPUA NEW GUINEA

C. York

Timor Sea

Melville I.

Darwin
Arnhem Land

C. Arnhem

Gulf of Carpentaria

Weipa
Cape York Peninsula

INDIAN OCEAN

Wyndham
Kimberley

Fitzroy

Broome

NORTHERN

Barkly Tableland

Cairns

Great Barrier Reef

Coral Sea

Tanami Desert

TERRITORY

Mount Isa

Townsville

Great Sandy Desert

Dampier

Hamersley Range

Mount Newman

Gibson Desert

Macdonnell Ranges

Alice Springs

QUEENSLAND

Great Divide

Tropic of Capricorn

Barcoo

Rockhampton

Bundaberg

Ayers Rock

Musgrave Ranges

WESTERN

Great Victoria Desert

AUSTRALIA

SOUTH

L. Eyre

AUSTRALIA

Charleville

Warrego

Brisbane
Toowoomba

Geraldton

Kalgoorlie-Boulder

L. Torrens

L. Gairdner

Flinders Ranges

NEW SOUTH

Darling

Nullarbor Plain

Broken Hill

WALES

Lachlan

Blue Mountains

Newcastle

Perth

Darling Range

Whyalla

Port Pirie

Murray

Murrumbidgee

Sydney

Great Australian Bight

Adelaide

Canberra

Wollongong

Cape Leeuwin

Albany

Kangaroo I.

VICTORIA

Mt. Kosciusko
2230

SOUTHERN OCEAN

Geelong

Melbourne

Australian Alps

Bass Strait

Launceston

TASMANIA

Hobart

Height of the land

over 6000 metres
4000 - 6000
2000 - 4000
1000 - 2000
400 - 1000
200 - 400
0 - 200 metres
below sea level

▲ Highest point on the map

sea level

Country boundaries
Large cities
Canberra Capital city underlined

Scale 1:20 000 000

0   200km   400km   600km   800km   1000km   1200km

1 cm on the map = 200 km on the ground

0   200miles   400miles   600miles   800miles

1 inch on the map = 320 miles on the ground

The Indian-Pacific Express

Town	Time	Day no.	Distance (kilometres)
Perth	21.00	1	0
Kalgoorlie	06.30	2	655
Port Pirie	10.25	3	2435
Adelaide	13.50	3	2657
Broken Hill	00.10	4	3223
Sydney	19.35	4	4345

It takes three nights and three days to cross Australia by train, from Perth to Sydney. The map shows you why the train is called the Indian-Pacific.

Australia is the world's largest island, but the smallest continent. It is the sixth-largest country in the world, smaller than the USA or Canada, but more than twice the size of India. Yet Australia has only about 17 million people. Most Australians are descended from people who came from Europe in the past 150 years.

The map shows that all the state capitals are on the coast, but Canberra, the national capital, is inland. Most Australians live in towns near the coast.

Only a few people live in the mountains or in the outback – the enormous area of semi-desert and desert that makes up most of the country. The few outback people live on huge sheep and cattle farms, in mining towns, or on special reserves for the original Australians, the Aborigines. Yet the wool, the meat, and the minerals of the outback are important exports.

▲ **The Great Barrier Reef** is the world's largest living thing! It is an area of coral over 2000 kilometres long, which grows in the warm sea near the coast of Queensland.

▲ **Ayers Rock** is in the heart of the desert in central Australia. Nothing grows on its steep sides. At sunset, it looks bright red!

Christmas 'down under' is in midsummer. Justine's stamp shows a typical Australian Christmas at the seaside, with swimming and sunbathing. But she didn't forget Father Christmas, with his red coat and his reindeer!

▼ **Animals in Australia.** Australia is not joined to any other continent. It has been a separate island for millions of years, and has developed its own unique wildlife.

▼ Four of these animals are endangered species: they will die out unless they are protected. Most of the world's marsupials live in Australia.

The first stamp for the whole of Australia showed the country's most famous animal. Kangaroos are marsupials – mother has her own 'pocket' for baby Roo! ▼

Australia 5c
Queensland Hairy-nosed Wombat
Endangered Species

Eastern Snake-necked Tortoise
AUSTRALIA 15c

Australia 25c
Greater Bilby
Endangered Species

Australia 30c

Smooth Knob-tailed Gecko
AUSTRALIA 40c

Australia 50c
Leadbeater's Possum
Endangered Species

AUSTRALIA POSTAGE
TWO PENCE HALFPENNY

NEW ZEALAND

The Antipodes

New Zealand is on the opposite side of the Earth from Europe. This double map shows that the far north of New Zealand is at the same latitude as North Africa, and that the far south of New Zealand is at the same latitude as Paris.

The New Zealand flag includes the British flag, because it was a British colony for over 100 years. Most New Zealand families originally came from Britain. The stars are known as the Southern Cross.

The two main islands that make up New Zealand are 2000 kilometres east of Australia. Only 3½ million people live in the whole country. The capital is Wellington, near the centre of New Zealand, but the largest city is Auckland in the north.

The original inhabitants were the Maoris, but now they are only about 8 per cent of the population. Some place-names are Maori words, such as Rotorua and Wanganui.

South Island is the largest island, but has fewer people than North Island. There are more sheep than people! Mount Cook, the highest point in New Zealand (3753 metres) is in the spectacular Southern Alps. Tourists visit the far south to see the glaciers and fjords. The fast-flowing rivers are used for hydro-electricity.

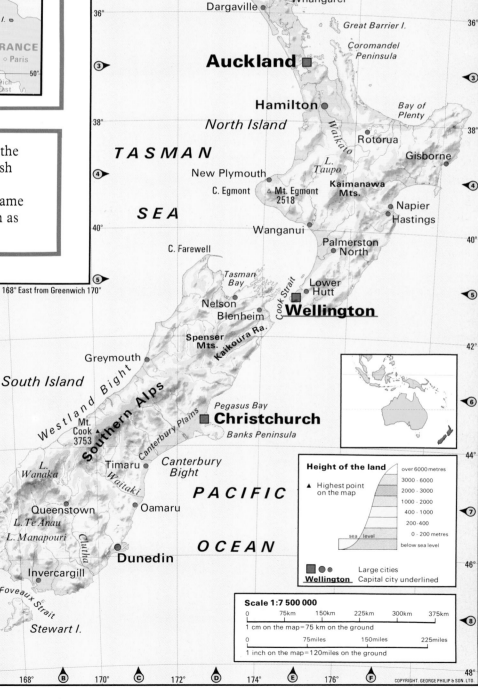

▼ *A geothermal power-station* on North Island. In *this volcanic area there is natural hot steam underground which can be piped to power-stations to produce electricity.*

North Island has a warmer climate than South Island. In some places you can see hot springs and boiling mud pools and there are also volcanoes. Fine trees and giant ferns grow in the forests, but much of the forest has been cleared for farming. Cattle are kept on the rich grasslands for meat and milk. Many different kinds of fruit grow well, including apples and kiwi-fruit.

New Zealand exports

These stamps show some major exports:
10c : pine trees become sawn timber for export;
18c : sheep's wool is spun for export;
20c : cattle hides and skins being lifted on to a ship;
25c : cartons of New Zealand butter being loaded.
Notice the snow-covered volcano in the background of the 25c stamp: this is Mount Egmont.

▼ *Sheep grazing on the Canterbury Plains,* on *South Island. New Zealand lamb is exported to Europe and North America in refrigerated ships. In the distance are the snow-covered Southern Alps. This great mountain range has glaciers, fjords and ski-slopes.*

ANTARCTICA

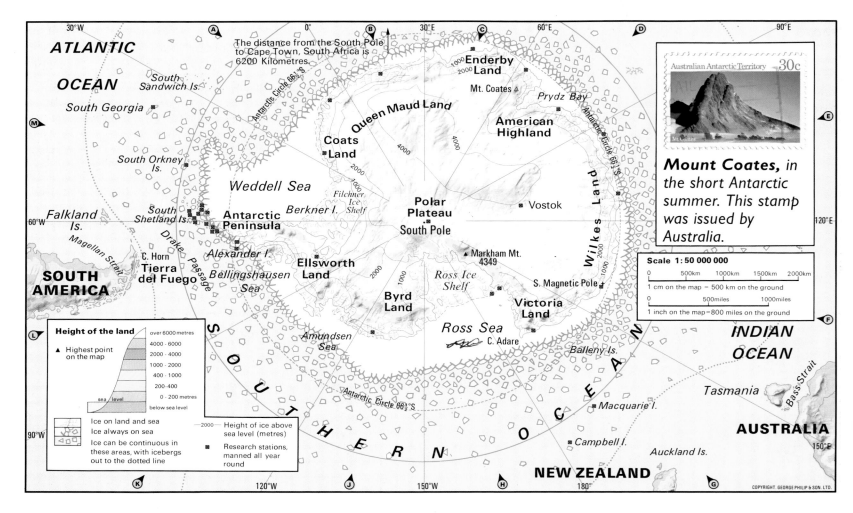

ATLANTIC OCEAN

The distance from the South Pole to Cape Town, South Africa is 6200 Kilometres.

South Sandwich Is.

South Georgia

Antarctic Circle 66½°S

Enderby Land

Mt. Coates

Prydz Bay

Queen Maud Land

American Highland

South Orkney Is.

Coats Land

Weddell Sea

Filchner Ice Shelf

Polar Plateau

Vostok

South Shetland Is.

Berkner I.

South Pole

Falkland Is.

Antarctic Peninsula

Magellan Strait

Drake Passage

Alexander I.

Ellsworth Land

Markham Mt. 4349

Wilkes Land

S. Magnetic Pole

SOUTH AMERICA

C. Horn Tierra del Fuego

Bellingshausen Sea

Byrd Land

Ross Ice Shelf

Victoria Land

Amundsen Sea

Ross Sea

C. Adare

Balleny Is.

INDIAN OCEAN

SOUTHERN

Antarctic Circle 66½°S

Tasmania

Bass Strait

Macquarie I.

AUSTRALIA

Campbell I.

Auckland Is.

NEW ZEALAND

Mount Coates, in the short Antarctic summer. This stamp was issued by Australia.

Australian Antarctic Territory 30c

Mt Coates

Scale 1 : 50 000 000

| 0 | 500km | 1000km | 1500km | 2000km |

1 cm on the map = 500 km on the ground

| 0 | 500miles | 1000miles |

1 inch on the map = 800 miles on the ground

Height of the land

▲ Highest point on the map

over 6000 metres
4000 - 6000
2000 - 4000
1000 - 2000
400 - 1000
200 - 400
0 - 200 metres

sea level

below sea level

Ice on land and sea
Ice always on sea
Ice can be continuous in these areas, with icebergs out to the dotted line

—2000— Height of ice above sea level (metres)

▨ Research stations, manned all year round

COPYRIGHT. GEORGE PHILIP & SON. LTD.

▼ **Emperor penguins** *with chicks. Penguins cannot fly, but they can swim very well. The parents use their feet to protect the eggs and chicks from the cold ice! No land animals live in Antarctica, but the ocean is full of fish, which provide food for penguins, seals and whales.*

Fact box: Antarctica

5th largest continent – about 13,900,000 square kilometres

Surrounded by cold **seas**
South Pole **first reached** in 1911

Antarctica is the continent surrounding the South Pole. It is the coldest, windiest and iciest place in the world! It is also very isolated, as the map shows.

No people live in Antarctica permanently. Some scientists work in research stations.

Everything that is needed in Antarctica has to be brought in during the short summer. From November to January, icebreakers can reach the land. But huge icebergs are always a danger. In winter (May to July) it is always dark, the sea is frozen, and people have to face extreme cold and dangerous blizzards.

ARCTIC

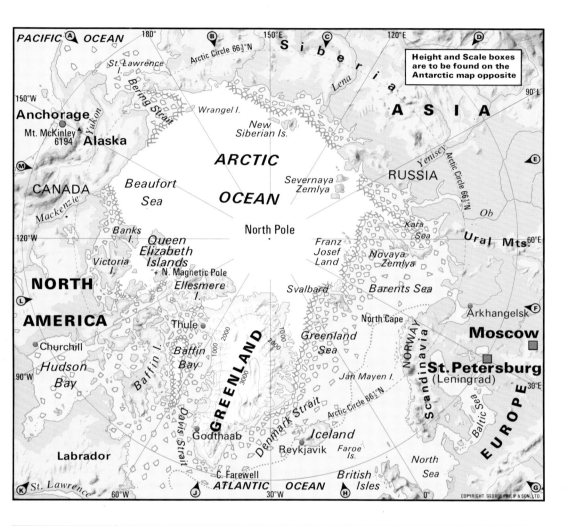

The Arctic is an ocean, which is frozen throughout the winter and still has lots of ice in summer. It is surrounded by the northernmost areas of three continents, but Greenland is the only truly Arctic country.

For most of the year the land is snow-covered. During the short summer, when the sun never sets, the snow and the frozen topsoil melt. But the deeper soil is still frozen, so the land is very marshy. This treeless landscape is called the tundra.

The reindeer and caribou can be herded or hunted, but farming is impossible. In recent years, rich mineral deposits have been found. Canada, the USA and Russia have military bases near the Arctic Ocean.

Fact box: Arctic

4th largest ocean – about 14,000,000 square kilometres

World record for least sunshine and tallest iceberg
Surrounded by cold **land**
North Pole **first reached** in 1909

▲ *Eskimos. The Inuit (Eskimos) have lived in the Arctic for thousands of years by hunting and fishing. The Inuit only build igloos as emergency shelters. Most of them live in wooden buildings that are well insulated against the cold, like the Greenland family (above), and most are more likely to travel by motorized skidoo than by sledge. Many work in mining camps, military bases and weather stations.*

◀ *These men are resting their husky dogs which are trained to pull sledges.*

QUIZ

▼ Name the island

The name of the continent where each island is found is marked on each outline. Do you know (*a*) the name of each island and (*b*) to which country each island belongs (or are they island countries)?

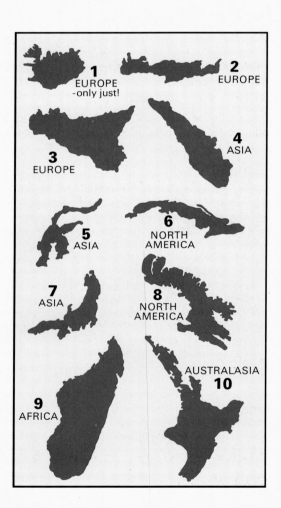

Oceans and seas

What ocean would you cross on an aeroplane journey . . .

1   From Australia to the USA?
2   From Brazil to South Africa?
3   From Canada to Russia?
4   From Madagascar to Indonesia?
5   From Mexico to Portugal?

▼ Name the country

There is a long, thin country in almost every continent. Can you name the countries shown here – and name the continent in which they are found? (If you need help, look at pages 8–9 for a map of the countries of the world.)

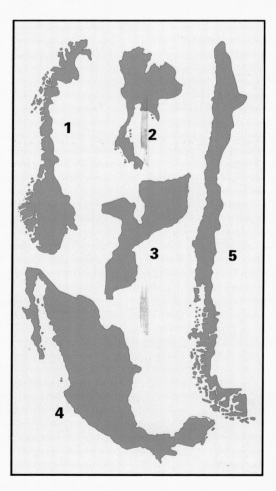

What sea would you cross on an aeroplane journey . . .

6   From Saudi Arabia to Egypt?
7   From Korea to Japan?
8   From Denmark to the UK?
9   From Vietnam to the Philippines?
10   From Cuba to Colombia?

A mystery message

Use the map of the countries of the world on pages 8–9 to decode this message. Each missing word is all or part of the name of a country. (For some answers, letters have to be taken out of or added to the name of the country.)

I was _ _ _ _ A_ _ (east of Austria), so I bought a large _ _ _ _ _ _ (east of Greece), some _ _ _ _ _ ns (east of Norway) and a bottle of _ _ _ _ ugal (west of Spain). Finally, I ate an _ _ _land (west of Norway) -cream. I enjoyed my _e_ _l (east of Mauritania), but afterwards I began to _ _ _ _ _enia (south of Romania) and I got a bad S_ _ _ _ (south of France). A O_ _ _ (east of Saudi Arabia) told me: 'Just eat Philip_ _ _ _apples (south of Taiwan) and _ _gypt (east of Libya), cooked in a Ja_ _ _ (east of Korea). Tomorrow you can eat a Ghban_ _ _ (east of Ivory Coast) and some _ _ _ _ _ _ (east of Peru) nuts. It shouldn't _ _ _ _ A Rica (west of Panama) you too much.' I said: 'You must be _ _ _ dagascar (east of Mozambique)! I think I've got _ _ _ _ yr_ _ (north of Indonesia). I'll have _ _ / _ _ (west of Benin) to a doctor quickly, otherwise I'll soon be _ _ _ _ Sea (lake between Israel and Jordan).' Happily, the doctor _ _ bared (island country south of USA) me, so I am still M_ _d_ _ _s (islands west of Sri Lanka) today!

Places in Asia

Move the letters to find:

Countries
RAIN; CHAIN; MOAN; AWAIT N.

Capital cities
ANIMAL; I HELD; A BULK
KEG NIP; LOUSE; DIARY H.

Find the colour

Each answer is a colour. Use the atlas index and the maps to help you. Cover the right-hand column with a piece of paper and try to answer the left-hand column only. Award yourself 2 points for each correct answer to the left-hand column only, or 1 point if you used the clues in both columns.

1 A sea between Egypt and Saudi Arabia. . .

2 A huge island east of Canada. . .

3 The sea between Turkey and Ukraine. . .

4 The sea between Korea and China. . .

5 The sea on which Arkhangelsk lies, in Russia. . .

6 A town in southern France which is also a fruit. . .

7 The tributary of the River Nile that flows from Ethiopia to Khartoum (Sudan). . .

. . . and the river on the border of Oklahoma and Texas, USA.

. . . and a bay on the west side of Lake Michigan, USA.

. . . and a forest in Germany.

. . . and a (stony) river in Wyoming, USA.

. . . and the river flowing north from Lake Victoria to Khartoum (Sudan).

. . . and the river which makes the border between South Africa and Namibia.

. . . and a mountain ridge in eastern USA.

How well do you know the states of the USA?

All the answers can be found on the maps on pages 62–3 and 66–9. Do not include Alaska and Hawaii.

1 Which is the *biggest* state?
2 Which is the *smallest* state?
3 Which state reaches furthest *north*? (careful!)
4 Which state reaches furthest *south*?
5 Which state reaches furthest *west*?
6 Which state reaches furthest *east*?
7 Which state is split into two by a lake?
8 Which state is split into two by an inlet of the sea?
9 Which two states are perfect rectangles in shape?
10 Which state is shaped like a saucepan?
11 In which state would you be if you visited Lake Huron?
12 In which state would you be if you visited Lake Ontario?
13 In which state would you be if you visited the Great Salt Lake?
14 In which state would you be if you visited the Mississippi delta?
15 Which state in *northern* USA is called South. . . . . .?
16 Which state in *southern* USA is called North. . . . . .?
17 There is only one place in the USA where four states meet: which states?
18 How many states have a border with Mexico?
19 How many states have a coastline on the Pacific?
20 How many states have a coastline on the Gulf of Mexico?

Great rivers of Europe

Use pages 18–37 to discover which great river flows through or near each pair of cities.
1 Vienna (Austria) and Budapest (Hungary).
2 Rotterdam (Netherlands) and Bonn (Germany).
3 Avignon (France) and Lyons (France).
4 Worcester (England) and Gloucester (England).
5 Toledo (Spain) and Lisbon (Portugal.)

Things To Do

Where do the things you use come from?

What do you and your family use, eat or wear from different countries of the world? In this atlas you will find lists of some items we have found (pages 27 and 37). Now you can do some spotting.

Collect stamps with a theme

A stamp collection soon grows. Try a *thematic* collection: choose a theme (topic) and collect stamps on that theme. For example, you could collect:
Flags on stamps. Togo had a flag stamp for Independence Day.

Map stamps: small islands often issue map stamps to show everyone where they are!

Traditional crafts on stamps: this Zambian thatcher is using a home-made ladder.

Make your own coin collection

Ask people who have been abroad for any foreign coins they do not want – you will have an instant collection! If you cannot have the coins to keep, you could make pencil or crayon rubbings on thin paper. Look at the pictures of coins in the atlas. Look at your coins for examples of languages; crops; famous buildings; historic events. . . .

INDEX

How to use this Index

The first number given after each name or topic is the page number; then a letter and another number tell you which square of the map you should look at.

For example, Abidjan is in square B2 on page 56. Find B at the top or the bottom of the map on page 56 and put a finger on it. Put another finger on the number 2 at the side of the map. Move your fingers in from the edge of the map and they will meet in square B2. Abidjan will now be easy to find. It is the capital city of the Ivory Coast, a country in West Africa.

If a name goes through more than one square, the square given in the Index is the one in which the biggest part of the name falls.

Names like *Gulf of Mexico* and *Cape Horn* are in the Index as *Mexico, Gulf of* and *Horn, Cape*.

93

Kenya 59 C2
Kerguelen 9 S5
Kermadec Islands 82 L11
Key West 69 C4
Khabarovsk 40 S3
Kharkov 36 F5
Khartoum 55 G3
Kiel 28 C1
Kiev 36 D4
Kigali 59 C3
Kikwit 59 A3
Kilimanjaro 59 C3
Kimberley (Australia) 84 E3
Kimberley (S. Africa) 61 B3
Kinabalu 46 C3
Kingston 74 C3
Kinshasa 59 A3
Kirghizia 40 L4
Kiribati 82 L8
Kiritimati Island 83 P8
Kirkenes 22 F2
Kirov 36 H3
Kiruna 22 E2
Kisangani 59 B2
Kishinev 36 D5
Kismayu 59 D3
Kiso, River 51 C3
Kisumu 59 C3
Kitakami, River 51 D3
Kitakyushu 51 A4
Kitwe 61 B2
Klagenfurt 28 F5
Kobe 51 B4
Koblenz 28 B3
Kola Peninsula 36 F1
Kolyma Range 40 U2
Korea Strait 51 A4
Kosciusko, Mount 84 J7
Krakatoa 46 B4
Krakow 36 C5
Krasnoyarsk 40 M3
Krishna, River 44 C3
Kristiansand 22 B4
Kuala Lumpur 46 B3
Kucing 46 C3
Kumamoto 51 B4
Kumasi 56 B2
Kunashir 51 E2
Kunlun Shan Mountains 48 B3
Kunming 48 D4
Kuopio 22 F3
Kuria Muria Islands 42 E4
Kuril Islands 82 J4
Kushiro 51 D2
Kuwait 42 D3
Kweilin 48 E4
Kweiyang 48 D4
Kyoga, Lake 59 C2
Kyoto 51 C3
Kyushu 51 B4

La Coruna 30 A2
La Paz 79 D4
La Plata 81 D3
La Rochelle 26 D3
La Spezia 33 C2
Labrador 65 M4
Laccadive Islands 44 C3
Lachlan, River 84 H6
Ladoga, Lake 36 E2
Lagos (Nigeria) 56 C2
Lagos (Portugal) 30 A5
Lahore 44 C1
Lakes 63, 66, 77
Lanchow 48 D3
Land's End 20 C5
Languedoc 26 F5
Laos 46 B2
Lapland 22 E2
Las Palmas 55 B2
Las Vegas 71 C3
Latvia 36 D3
Launceston 84 J8
Lausanne 33 A1
Lauterbrunnen 33 B1
Le Havre 26 D2

Le Mans 26 D2
Lebanon 42 C2
Leeds 20 F4
Leeuwarden 24 D1
Leeuwin, Cape 84 B6
Leiden 24 C2
Leipzig 28 E3
Lek, River 24 C3
Lena, River 40 R2
Lens 26 F1
Leon (Mexico) 73 B2
Leon (Spain) 30 C2
Lerida 30 F3
Lesotho 61 B3
Lesser Antilles 74 F4
Lewis 20 C1
Lhasa 48 C4
Liberia 56 B2
Libreville 56 D2
Libya 55 E2
Libyan Desert 55 F2
Liechtenstein 28 D5
Liège 24 D4
Ligurian Sea 33 B3
Likasi 59 B4
Lille 26 F1
Lillehammer 22 B3
Lilongwe 61 C2
Lima 79 C4
Limassol 42 J2
Limoges 26 E4
Limpopo, River 61 B3
Linares 30 D4
Line Islands 83 P9
Linz 28 F4
Lions, Gulf of 26 G5
Lipari Islands 33 E5
Lisbon 30 A4
Lithuania 36 D3
Liverpool 20 E4
Livingstone 61 B2
Ljubljana 35 A1
Llanos 79 C2
Lobito 61 A2
Lodz 36 B4
Lofer 28 E5
Lofoten Islands 22 C2
Logan, Mount 65 E3
Loire, River 26 E3
Lome 56 C2
London (Canada) 65 K5
London (U.K.) 20 G5
Londonderry 20 C3
Lorient 26 C3
Lorraine 26 H2
Los Angeles 71 B3
Louisiana 66
Louisville 69 C3
Lourdes 26 E6
Lower California 73 A2
Lower Hutt 86 E5
Lualaba, River 59 B3
Luanda 61 A1
Lubango 61 A2
Lübeck 28 D2
Lubumbashi 59 B4
Lucknow 44 D2
Lugano 33 B1
Luzern 33 B1
Lule, River 22 E2
Lulea 22 E2
Lusaka 61 B2
Luton 20 F5
Luxembourg 24 E5
Luzon 46 D2
Lvov 36 D5
Lyons 26 G4

Maas, River 24 D3
Maastricht 24 D4
Macao 48 E4
Macdonnell Ranges 84 E4
Macedonia 35 C2
Machu Picchu 79 C4
Mackenzie River 65 F3
Macquarie Island 88 G
Madagascar 61 D3

Madeira 55 B1
Madeira, River 79 C2
Madras 44 D3
Madrid 30 C3
Madurai 44 C4
Magadan 40 T2
Magdalena, River 79 C2
Magdeburg 28 E2
Magellan's Strait 81 C5
Mahajanga 61 D2
Maiduguri 56 D1
Main, River 28 D3
Maine 66
Majorca 30 G4
Makasar Strait 46 C4
Makgadikgadi Salt Pan 61 B3
Malacca, Straits of 46 B3
Malaga 30 C5
Malawi 61 C2
Malawi, Lake 61 C2
Malay Peninsula 38 P8
Malaysia 46 B3
Maldives 44 C4
Mali 55 C3
Malmo 22 C4
Malta 33 E6
Man, Isle of 20 D3
Manaar, Gulf of 44 C4
Manado 46 D3
Managua 73 D3
Manapouri, Lake 86 B7
Manaus 79 D3
Manchester 20 E4
Manchuria 48 F2
Mandalay 46 A1
Manila 46 C2
Manitoba 65 J4
Mannheim 28 C4
Maps 16-17
Maputo 61 C3
Maracaibo 79 C2
Margarita 74 F4
Maria van Diemen, Cape 86 C2
Mariana Trench 82 H7
Market 25, 27, 47, 54, 56, 62
Markham, Mount 88 G
Marquesas Islands 83 R9
Marrakesh 55 B1
Marseilles 26 G5
Marshall Islands 82 L7
Martinique 74 F4
Maryland 66
Maseru 61 B3
Mashhad 42 E2
Massachusetts 66
Massif Central 26 F4
Matadi 59 A3
Mato Grosso plateau 79 E4
Matsuyama 51 B4
Maui 66 G1
Mauna Kea 66 G2
Mauna Loa 66 G2
Mauritania 55 B3
Mauritius 9 S4
Mbabane 61 C3
Mbandaka 59 A2
Mbeya 59 C3
Mbini 56 D2
Mbuji-Mayi 59 B3
McKinley, Mount 66 C2
Mecca 42 C3
Medan 46 A3
Medellin 79 C2
Medicine Hat 65 G5
Medina 42 C3
Mediterranean Sea 18 K7
Mekong, River 46 B2
Melanesia 82 J9
Melbourne 84 J7
Melilla 30 D6
Melville Island (Canada) 65 G2
Melville Islands (Australia) 84 E2
Memphis 69 C3

Mendoza 81 C3
Mentawai Islands 46 A4
Meseta 30 C4
Mesopotamia 42 D2
Messina (Italy) 33 E5
Messina (South Africa) 61 C3
Metz 26 H2
Meuse, River 24 D4
Mexico 73 B2
Mexico City 73 B3
Mexico, Gulf of 73 D2
Miami 69 D4
Michigan 66
Michigan, Lake 69 C2
Micronesia 82 K8
Mindanao 46 D3
Minho, River 30 A2
Milan 33 B2
Milwaukee 69 B2
Minneapolis 69 B2
Minnesota 66
Minorca 30 G4
Minsk 36 D4
Mississippi River 69 B3
Mississippi State 66
Missouri State 66
Mitchell, Mount 69 C3
Mjosa Lake 22 C3
Mobutu Sese Seko, Lake 59 B2
Mogadishu 59 D2
Moldavia 36 D5
Molokai 66 F1
Molucca Sea 46 D4
Mombasa 59 D3
Monaco 26 H5
Mongolia 48 D2
Mongu 61 B2
Monrovia 56 A2
Mons 24 B4
Monsoon 45
Montana 66
Montbéliard 26 H3
Montego Bay 74 C3
Montenegro 35 B2
Monterrey 73 B2
Montevideo 81 D3
Montgomery 69 C3
Montpellier 26 F6
Montreal 65 L5
Montserrat 74 F3
Moon 4
Moorea 83 Q10
Morava, River 35 C2
Morena, Sierra 30 C4
Morocco 55 C1
Moscow 36 F3
Moselle, River 26 H2
Moshi 59 C3
Mosul 42 D2
Moulmein 46 A2
Mount Isa 84 G4
Mount Newman 84 D4
Mount Pilatus 33 B1
Mozambique 61 C2
Mozambique Channel 61 D2
Mulhacen 30 D5
Mulhouse 26 H3
Mull 20 C2
Multan 44 C1
Munich 28 D4
Münster 28 B3
Muonio, River 22 E2
Mur, River 28 F5
Murcia 30 E5
Murmansk 36 F1
Murray, River 84 H6
Murrumbidgee, River 84 J6
Musala 35 C2
Muscat 42 E3
Musgrave Ranges 84 F5
Mutare 61 C2
Mwanza 59 C3
Mweru, Lake 59 B3

Nafud Desert 42 D3
Nagasaki 51 A4
Nagoya 51 C3
Nagpur 44 D2
Nairobi 59 C3
Namib Desert 61 A3
Namibia 61 A3
Namur 24 C4
Nan Shan Mountains 48 C3
Nanching 48 E4
Nancy 26 G2
Nandi 59 C2
Nanking 48 E3
Nantes 26 D3
Nao, Cabo de la 30 F4
Napier 86 F4
Naples 33 D4
Nara 51 C4
Narmada, River 44 C2
Narvik 22 D2
Nashville 69 C3
Nassau 74 C1
Nasser, Lake 55 G2
Nauru 82 K9
Nazare 30 A3
Nazareth 42 M2
Ndjamena 55 E3
Ndola 61 B2
Neagh, Lough 20 C3
Nebraska 66
Negro, River 79 D3
Neisse, River 28 F3
Nelson 86 D5
Nelson, River 65 J4
Nemuro Strait 51 E2
Nepal 44 D2
Netherlands 24 E2
Nevada 66
Nevada, Sierra 30 D5
New Brunswick 65 M5
New Caledonia 82 K11
New Castile 30 D4
New Guinea 82 H9
New Hampshire 66
New Jersey 66
New Mexico 66
New Orleans 69 C4
New Plymouth 86 D4
New Siberian Islands 40 U1
New South Wales 84 J6
New York 69 D2
New York State 66
New Zealand 86
Newcastle (Australia) 84 K6
Newcastle (U.K.) 20 E3
Newfoundland 65 N5
Ngorongoro 59 C3
Niagara Falls 65 L5
Niamey 56 C1
Nicaragua 73 D3
Nice 26 H5
Nicobar Islands 46 A3
Nicosia 42 J1
Niger 55 C3
Niger, River 56 C1
Nigeria 56 C2
Niigata 51 C3
Nijmegen 24 D3
Nile, River 55 G2
Nîmes 26 G5
Nis 35 C2
Nizhniy Novgorod 36 H3
Nome 66 B2
Norfolk 69 D3
Normandy 26 E5
Norrkoping 22 D4
North America 62
North Cape 22 E1
North Carolina 66
North Dakota 66
North European plain 18 L4
North Island, New Zealand 86 D4
North Korea 48 F3
North Magnetic Pole 89 L
North Pole 89
North Sea 18 H3

North West Highlands 20 D2
North West Territories 65 H3
Northampton 20 F4
Northern Ireland 20 C3
Northern Territory 84 F3
Norway 22 C3
Norwich 20 G4
Nottingham 20 F4
Nouakchott 55 B3
Nova Scotia 65 M5
Novaya Zemlya 40 J1
Novosibirsk 40 N3
Nullarbor Plain 84 E6
Nuremberg 28 D4

Oahua 66 F1
Oamaru 86 C7
Ob, River 40 K2
Oban 20 D2
Oceans 6-7, 82
Odense 22 C4
Oder, River 28 F2
Odessa 36 E5
Ogbomosho 56 C2
Ogooue, River 56 D3
Ohio 66
Ohio River 69 C3
Oil 43
Okavango Swamp 61 B2
Okayama 51 B4
Okhotsk, Sea of 40 T3
Oki Islands 51 B3
Oklahoma 66
Oklahoma City 71 D3
Oland 22 D4
Old Castile 30 D3
Oldenburg 28 B2
Omaha 69 B2
Oman 42 E3
Oman, Gulf of 42 E3
Omdurman 55 F3
Omsk 40 L3
Onega, Lake 36 F2
Onega, River 36 F2
Ontario 65 L5
Ontario, Lake 69 D2
Oporto 30 A3
Oran 55 D1
Orange 26 G4
Orange River 61 A3
Ore Mountains 28 E3
Orebro 22 C4
Oregon 66
Orenburg 36 K4
Orense 30 B2
Orinoco, River 79 D2
Orkney Islands 20 E1
Orléans 26 E3
Osaka 51 C4
Oslo 22 B4
Ostend 24 A3
Ostersund 22 D3
Otaru 51 D2
Otranto, Strait of 33 G4
Ottawa 65 L5
Ouagadougou 56 B1
Oulu 22 F2
Oulu, Lake 22 F3
Oviedo 30 B2
Oxford 20 F5

Pacific Ocean 82 L7
Padang 46 B4
Padua 33 C2
Pakistan 44 B2
Palawan 46 C2
Palembang 46 B4
Palermo 33 D5
Palm Beach 69 D4
Palma 30 G4
Palmerston North 86 E5
Pampas 81 C3

Pamplona 30 E2
Panama 73 E4
Panama Canal 73 D3
Pantellaria 33 D6
Paotow 48 D2
Papua New Guinea 82 H9
Paraguay 81 D2
Paramaribo 79 E2
Parana River 81 D2
Paris 26 F2
Parma 33 C2
Patagonia 81 C4
Patrai 35 C3
Peace River 65 G4
Pegasus Bay 86 D6
Peking 48 E2
Pemba 59 D3
Pennines 20 E3
Pennsylvania 66
Penzance 20 D5
Perm 36 K3
Perpignan 26 F6
Perth (Australia) 84 B6
Perth (U.K.) 20 E2
Peru 79 C4
Perugia 33 D3
Pescara 33 D3
Philadelphia 69 D3
Philippines 46 C2
Phnom Penh 46 B2
Phoenix 71 B3
Phoenix Islands 82 M9
Picardy 26 F2
Pindus Mountains 35 C3
Pisa 33 C3
Pitcairn Island 83 R11
Pittsburgh 69 C2
Plains 6, 18, 39, 71
Plata, Rio de la 81 D3
Plateau 49, 60
Plates 5
Plenty, Bay of 86 F3
Ploesti 35 D2
Plovdiv 35 D2
Plymouth 20 E5
Po, River 33 C2
Pointe-Noire 59 A3
Poitiers 26 E3
Poland 36 B4
Polar lands 12-13, 88-9
Polar Plateau 88 C
Polynesia 83 N8
Pontianak 46 C4
Poopo, Lake 79 D4
Port Elizabeth 61 B4
Port Harcourt 56 C2
Port of Spain 74 F4
Port Pirie 84 G6
Port Said 55 G1
Port Sudan 55 G3
Port Talbot 20 D5
Port-au-Prince 74 D3
Portland 71 A2
Porto Alegre 79 F5
Portsmouth 20 F5
Portugal 30 B4
Potsdam 28 E2
Prague 36 B4
Pretoria 61 B3
Prince Edward Island 65 M5
Prince Edward Islands 9 P5
Prince George 65 G4
Prince Rupert 65 F4
Pripet, River 36 D4
Provence 26 G5
Providence 69 D2
Prudhoe Bay 66 C2
Prut, River 35 D1
Prydz Bay 88 D
Puebla 73 C3
Pueblo 71 C3
Puerto Rico 74 E3
Pune 44 C3
Punta Arenas 81 B5
Pusan 48 G3
Pyongyang 48 F3
Pyrenees 30 F2

ANSWERS TO QUESTIONS

Answers to text questions

page 18 Western Europe's most important building: the Headquarters of the European Community in Brussels, the capital of Belgium. In this building many of the important decisions about Western Europe are made. The photograph shows reflections in the double-glazed windows. In the reflection you can see small old houses and shops and big modern office buildings in Brussels, the biggest city in Belgium.

page 19 B = Belgium; D = Germany (Deutschland in German); DK = Denmark; E = Spain (España); F = France; GB = Great Britain; GR = Greece; I = Italy; IRL = Ireland (Republic of Ireland); L = Luxembourg; NL = Netherlands; P = Portugal.

page 21 The London landmarks featured on the stamp are *(left to right)*: Westminster Abbey; Nelson's column (in Trafalgar Square); statue of Eros in Piccadilly Circus; Telecom Tower; clock tower of the Houses of Parliament (containing the bell Big Ben); St Paul's Cathedral; Tower Bridge; White Tower of the Tower of London.

page 25 Belgium has two official languages, French and Flemish. The coin on the left has the French name for Belgium, that on the right its Flemish name.

page 27 The vegetables on the stall are green and red peppers, aubergines, onions and tomatoes, with some cucumbers and baby marrows on the left.

page 29 The international clock in Berlin; the names on the clock stay still; the numbers move slowly round. In 24 hours, the numbers have turned a full circle –

just like the Earth in space! When the photograph was taken, at 16.00 hours (4 pm) in Berlin, it was 13.30 hours (1.30 pm) in Reykjavik, Iceland, and 17.00 hours (5 pm) in Helsinki, Finland. In places *west* of Berlin it is earlier in the day; in places *east* of Berlin, it is later in the day. Note the names on the clock are in German.

page 55 Puzzle picture: the circles are 'drawn' by huge centre-pivot irrigation sprays, which turn slowly to make the shape of a circle. Each circle is about 1 kilometre across. The irrigation allows crops to grow in the desert. Some of the crops in the circular 'fields' are already ripening, so they look less green.

page 57 Puzzle picture: this farmer in Ghana is making a mound of earth over each yam tuber he has planted.

page 62 The photograph of the fruit market shows *(at back)* bananas, pineapple; *(centre)* breadfruit, mango, lime; *(at front)* grapefruit, lemons, pawpaw, pineapple. There are vegetables on display behind.

page 63 The north shores of Lakes Superior, Huron, Erie and Ontario are in Canada, and the south shores in the USA. Lake Michigan is entirely in the USA.

page 63 El Salvador only has a coastline on the Pacific Ocean. Belize only has a coatline on the Caribbean Sea. (Honduras has a tiny coastline on the Pacific – look closely at the map!)

page 67 Seattle to Miami is 5445 kilometres; New Orleans to Chicago is 1488 kilometres.

page 69 The stamp shows the Mississippi River. It flows southwards to New Orleans and the Gulf of Mexico. It was used for transport far into the heart of America long before roads were built, so it became known as the 'Great River Road'.

Answers to quiz

Name the island
(Name of country in brackets after name of island)
1 Iceland (Iceland); 2 Crete (Greece); 3 Sicily (Italy); 4 Sumatra (Indonesia); 5 Sulawesi (Indonesia); 6 Cuba (Cuba); 7 Honshu (Japan); 8 Baffin Island (Canada); 9 Madagascar (Madagascar); 10 North Island (New Zealand).

Name the country
(Name of continent in brackets after name of country)
1 Norway (Europe);
2 Thailand (Asia);
3 Mozambique (Africa);
4 Mexico (Central America);
5 Chile (South America).

A mystery message
I was *hungry*, so I bought a large *turkey*, some *swedes* and a bottle of *port*. Finally, I ate an *ice-cream*. I enjoyed my meal, but afterwards I began to *bulge* and I got a bad *pain*. A man told me: 'Just eat *pine*apples and *egg* cooked in a *pan*. Tomorrow you can eat a *banana* and some *Brazil* nuts. It shouldn't *cost* you too much.' I said: 'You must be *mad*! I think I've got *malaria*. I'll have *to go* to a doctor quickly, otherwise I'll soon be *dead*.'

Happily, the doctor *cured* me, so I am still *alive* today!

Oceans and seas
1 Pacific; 2 Atlantic; 3 Arctic; 4 Indian; 5 Atlantic; 6 Red Sea; 7 Sea of Japan; 8 North Sea; 9 South China Sea; 10 Caribbean Sea.

Places in Asia
Countries Iran; China; Oman; Taiwan.
Capital cities Manila; Delhi; Kabul; Peking; Seoul; Riyadh.

Colour quiz
1 Red (Red Sea/Red River);
2 Green (Greenland/Green Bay);
3 Black (Black Sea/Black Forest);
4 Yellow (Yellow Sea/Yellowstone River);
5 White (White Sea/White Nile);
6 Orange (Orange/Orange River);
7 Blue (Blue Nile/Blue Ridge, USA).

Score for Colour quiz
13–14 Brilliant! 10–12 Very good. 6–9 Good. 2–5 Use this atlas more – you'll soon do better. 0–1 Try another planet – there's less geography there.

States of the USA
1 Texas; 2 Rhode Island; 3 Minnesota; 4 Florida; 5 California; 6 Maine; 7 Michigan; 8 Maryland; 9 Wyoming and Colorado; 10 Oklahoma; 11 Michigan; 12 New York; 13 Utah; 14 Louisiana; 15 South Dakota; 16 North Carolina; 17 Utah, Colorado, Arizona and New Mexico; 18 Four; 19 Three; 20 Five.

Great rivers of Europe
1 Danube; 2 Rhine; 3 Rhône; 4 Severn; 5 Tagus.

Illustration Acknowledgements

The Australian Tourist Commission p. 85 (top); **Bruce Coleman Limited** pp. 6, 8, 11 (right), 15 (left), 21 (below right), 23 (above right), 27 (top), 29 (below left), 32 (below), 37 (top), 38, 41 (below), 54 (top), 59, 61 (right), 69 (above left), 70 (top left and below), 72 (top), 78 (top), 80 (below), 82, 83, 87, 89 (below); **The Daily Telegraph** p. 5; **Susan Griggs** pp. 11 (left), 21 (top), 23 (below right), 31 (top), 33, 40, 41 (top), 42 (right), 43 (top), 45 (below), 50 (above left), 62, 63, 65 (right), 67, 70 (top right), 72 (below), 73, 76; **Robert Harding Picture Library** pp. 15 (right), 19, 39, 45 (centre), 47 (top), 49 (centre and below left), 50 (below), 58 (below left), 61 (left), 64 (left), 75 (top left), 78 (below left), 88; **The J. Allan Cash Photolibrary** pp. 12, 25 (below right and back cover), 29 (right), 31 (below left), 45 (top), 48, 50 (above right), 54 (below left), 56 (and back cover), 57 (top left), 58 (top and below right), 75 (below), 78 (below right); **NASA** p.55 (below left); **The Quentin Bell Organisation** p. 64 (right); **Ralph Somerville** p. 49 (top); **Spanish National Tourist Office** p. 31 (centre); **Vautier-de-Nanxe** pp. 42 (left), 71, 77, 80 (top), 81; **David and Jill Wright** pp. 10, 14, 16, 18, 21 (below right), 22, 23 (below left), 25 (top and below left), 27 (centre and below), 29 (top) 31 (below right), 34 (left), 35, 43 (below), 44, 52, 54 (below right), 57 (top right, centre and below), 60, 68 (above), 69 (centre and top right), 75 (top right), 85 (centre); **Louise Wright** p. 47 (below left); **Zefa** pp. 11 (centre), 20, 23 (above left), 24, 28, 32 (top), 34 (right), 37 (below, right and left), 53, 55 (below right), 65 (left), 68 (below), 79, 89 (centre).